ASK ABOUT
FLORIDA

Other books by James J. Raciti from Sunstone Press

PULLING NO PONCHOS

OLD SANTA FE

ASK ABOUT

Five hundred and thirty-eight questions
and their answers about the State of Florida from its origins to
the present day cover such subjects as the Native Americans,
the Spanish explorers, wars for dominance, the history of religion, politics,
population, resources, wildlife and remarkable people that lent their
imagination, hard work and dedication to the state.

FLORIDA

James J. Raciti

Library of Congress Cataloging-in-Publication Data

Raciti, James J., 1933-
    Ask about Florida / James J. Raciti.
        p. cm.
    ISBN 0-86534-456-6 (softcover)
    1. Florida—Miscellanea. I. Title.

F311.5.R33 2005
975.9—dc22
        2004027292

WWW.SUNSTONEPRESS.COM
SUNSTONE PRESS / POST OFFICE BOX 2321 / SANTA FE, NM 87504-2321 /USA
(505) 988-4418 / *ORDERS ONLY* (800) 243-5644 / FAX (505) 988-1025

Contents

Introduction

This book was written with various readers in mind. It is first for those local readers who may want a handy and easy-to-read review of historical events, and other useful information about the state. Then there are those visitors to Florida who may want to get an overall grasp on how the state grew from its origins in the fifteen hundreds to the present day. Many may want to compare Florida's development with those of other states that grew under the Spanish domination. The format is one of questions and answers. Those who know quite a bit about Florida may wish to test their knowledge and score their correct answers. Others may find that short bits of information can more easily be absorbed than pages upon pages of data. *Ask About Florida* provides this format.

Prior to the era of air-conditioned lifestyles, when Florida was still a very hot, humid and mosquito-infested peninsula, only the curious and the hardy moved to its shores. The French Huguenots settled in the northeast section of the state in search of religious tolerance but the Spanish drove them off. The English, always seeking to extend their influence from the north, were in constant conflict with Spain. As Floridians began to tame their environment, many more settlers came to build homes and farm the land. It was not until the 1800s that the railways pushed the borders of northern Florida to the south. The 1920s saw an enormous influx of immigrants, buying land)and making Florida their home. Many may feel that in the attempt to take what Americans truly felt was their due, they may not have treated the natives with sufficient concern. It has only been recently that we have become more sensitive to the cultural and religious differences and indeed the rights of the Indians. It is anyone's guess how we would have done it differently, had we been more caring of the sentiments of others. Manifest Destiny gave us a platform for believing that it was God's will that we invade and take over the entire landmass from the Atlantic Ocean to the Pacific. It has only been relatively recently for example, that we have questioned the actions of Andrew Jackson and his treatment of the Seminole Indians.

The Land

1. At the time when dinosaurs roamed across the North American Continent, what was happening on the peninsula we call today "Florida?"

Nothing. The landmass we call "Florida" was still submerged under the sea. Although Florida was an early discovery by European adventurers, it was a latecomer in geological terms.

2. What are the simple divisions of Florida?

Florida can be divided into two main sections: The Panhandle and The Peninsula. The Panhandle is the narrow strip of land that stretches along the Gulf Coast, south of Alabama and Georgia. The Peninsula stretches south along the Atlantic and the Gulf of Mexico for about four hundred miles.

3. Are there specific geographical regions in the state?

Florida can be divided into three natural geographical regions: the hardwood forests, the pine barrens and the wetlands.

4. What do geologists tell us about the makeup of the landmass in the state?

It is speculated that the flat, limestone-covered finger of land may not have been part of the North American continent but may have been part of the Bahamas and Cuba.

5. Has the climate in Florida always been as it is today?

The climate changed gradually from the Ice Age (9000 B.C.) to about 3000 B.C. at which time the climate stabilized and is not so different than it is today.

6. What is the average annual precipitation for the state?

Since there is practically no snow in Florida, the precipitation comes from abundant rainfall, which averages 54 inches annually.

7. Why is Florida especially prone to hurricanes?

Temperatures in Florida are high in the summer. Hurricanes form in the late summer when the sun heats the moist air over the ocean. This creates a rising spiral motion, which begins as a tropical storm.

8. Which Florida city has more thunderstorms than any other city in the United States?

Records show that Fort Myers is the leading city in the States for thunderstorms with about 100 days annually.

9. Where and when were the strongest winds recorded on the Atlantic Coast?

The year was 1935. It was a Labor Day hurricane in the Florida Keys. The winds were strong enough to blow railway cars off their tracks, and killed more than 400 people.

10. What are the extremes of temperature recorded for Florida?

The lowest recorded temperature for the state was minus two degrees Fahrenheit in Tallahassee. The highest temperature was 107 degrees in Monticello.

11. Why is the weather in the Florida Keys so special to Floridians?

Winter is typically ten degrees Fahrenheit warmer than on the Florida mainland; summer is usually ten degrees cooler. There is also less rain by half—30 inches annually—than on the mainland.

12. Many visitors seek out the climate of Florida for vacations. Are there disadvantages to the climate of the state?

Advantages like disadvantages can be subjective considerations but most people complain about the mildew, the flying insects and a variety of dangerous snakes—the water moccasin, the rattlesnake, the copperheads, etc.

13. How many miles of coastline does Florida claim?

Florida has 1,350 miles of coastline.

14. According to the Spanish explorers, what were the dimensions of the land they called "La Florida?"

The Spanish considered Florida to extend west to Texas and north to the Chesapeake region.

15. How many lakes are spread throughout the state?

There are more than 7,800 lakes ranging in size from one acre to 448,000 acres.

16. How many species of plant life have been cataloged in Florida?

Approximately 3500 species of plant life have been found in the state. Only Texas and California have more.

17. Where are the wetlands in Florida?

A century ago, a good bit of the state was under water. There are wetlands today along the Gulf Coast south of Tallahassee but mostly in central and south Florida.

18. Where are the hardwood forests in the state?

Northern Florida, with its higher elevation and richer soil has such hardwood trees as: hickory, holly, beech, maple, oak and magnolia.

19. What kind of soil supports the pine forests?

The soil that supports the pine trees is dry and sandy. This is the makeup of most of Central Florida's landmass. Aside from pine trees, there are scrub oaks and palmettos.

20. What is the largest of Florida's national forests?

The Apalachicola National Forest is the largest. It covers more than one-half million acres. The forest is home to many animals; among them are the wild pig and the black bear.

21. How is the sand along the coastline of the Panhandle different from that of the rest of the peninsula?

The sand along the coast throughout Florida is comprised of as many as twenty different minerals from crushed shells and coral. It is rough grained and holds moisture. The sand on the beaches of the Panhandle is very fine and has the texture of sugar. It's made of crushed quartz, which geologists say, washed down from the Appalachian Mountains.

22. Why are the beaches in and around Venice, Florida gray in color?

This is due to the large amounts of organic compounds in the sand called phosphates. When the sand is tan in color, it is a sign of a high shell and iron content.

23. What makes the Panama City coastline of interest to underwater life?

There are many natural reefs there as well as several dozen artificial reefs. In addition, there are many historical wrecks such as a World War II British tanker sunk by German submarines.

24. How did the cluster of coral reef islands west of Key West get the name of "Dry Tortugas?"

The early Spanish explorers named them. They were called "seca" meaning "dry" because there was no fresh water on these islands. They were named "Tortugas" meaning "turtles" for the hundreds of turtles they found there.

25. How big is the Everglades National Park?

It covers more than one million acres. It is made up of saw grass prairies, mangrove swamps and the warm waters of Florida Bay.

26. What is the solid ground made up of in the Everglades?

The bedrock is made up of limestone, formed from the remains of seashells and coral.

27. What are the seasons in the Everglades?

There are only two seasons: the wet season in summer and the dry season in winter. Rainfall in summer can reach twelve inches in a single day. During the winter, the water recedes and settles into ponds.

28. What was the purpose in draining the area just south of Lake Okeechobee?

The primary purpose was to create land that could be developed and farmed.

29. With the draining of the Everglades, what was planted in the rich soil that was reclaimed?

South of Lake Okeechobee is one of the most productive areas in the nation for sugarcane. Florida is the country's top producer of sugarcane and second only to California in the production of vegetables such as tomatoes, corn, beans and peppers.

30. Where is Lake Okeechobee?

The lake lies in South Central Florida. It is one of the nation's largest lakes. It is the largest of more than thirty thousand fresh water lakes and ponds in Florida.

31. What do visitors find of interest in Lake Okeechobee?

The lake is a bass fisherman's paradise. More than three million pounds of fish are caught here each year.

32. What brought a halt to the effort to reclaim the Everglades under state auspices?

In 1926, the Florida land boom collapsed. Funds were used up and the financial burden connected with the reclaiming of the Everglades was too great.

33. What negative results became apparent with drying out part of the Everglades?

Rainwater moves too quickly towards the Atlantic Ocean, creating a dangerously dry winter season, which is more prone to wildfires.

34. What is the strange tree in the Everglades called the "tourist tree?"

This is the gumbo-limbo tree. Its peeling red bark looks like a tourist's skin that has remained too long in the hot sun.

35. What Florida tree, mostly seen on the southern coast, is able to thrive on water and salt?

The mangrove tree thrives on a high content of salt and virtually lives in the high and low tides of the sea.

36. Why does Spanish moss grow so abundantly in Florida?

This moss, part of the bromeliaceae group, loves moist heat. It attaches itself on trees but does not send down roots. It lives on nourishment from photosynthesis and the water it takes from the air.

37. What is a Tung Tree?

It is a native of China, which produces a nut-like seed from which tung oil is extracted. It is used in quick-drying paint oil. The first tung tree was planted in Tallahassee in 1906. Within fifty years, 40,000 acres of Leon County had tung trees growing.

38. How does the Strangled Fig Tree get its sustenance?

This tree starts as a seed, which buries itself in another tree or host. It sends its roots into the soil near the host tree and begins to twist itself around until it kills the host tree.

39. How many islands are there within the state's boundaries?

Florida has 4,510 islands, not counting those smaller than ten acres. In the United States, only Alaska has more islands.

40. What is the largest river in Florida?

Of the thirty-four major rivers, St. Johns is the largest. It starts near Melbourne and flows 275 miles to Jacksonville. It is one of the few rivers in the United States that runs from south to north.

41. Is there really a river called "Suwannee?"

Yes. It is one of the better known of Florida's rivers. It lies in the northern part of the state and was made famous by Stephen Foster's song "Old Folks at Home."

42. Where is the largest limestone artesian spring formation in Florida?

Silver Springs, near Ocala, is the largest such formation in the world. Its daily average output is 800 million gallons. Early

Americans considered the location sacred. The site has had human habitation for more than 100 centuries.

43. What is the Devil's Mill Hopper?

This is a well-known sinkhole in Gainesville. It is 118 feet deep and 500 feet wide. This is the effect of the limestone eroding; then the ground beneath collapses. The hole then fills up with water. Sinkholes can become very large and dangerous.

44. Where did Florida's sponge industry get its start?

Key West had a large sponge market in the late 1800s. Greek-Americans brought their skills to the Tarpon Springs area later to build up that area in the sponge industry.

45. What was the original name given to the Florida Keys?

The Spanish explorers referred to those islands as "Los Martires" (The Martyrs), perhaps because they looked like a string of pain-stricken men.

46. What main factors contribute to the ideal farming conditions in northern Florida?

It has relatively warm climate, regular seasons, is free of destructive storms and has abundant rainfall.

47. What are the main crops of the Tallahassee area and Leon County?

The main crops now are sweet potato, corn and cotton.

48. When did the old plantation economy come to an end in Florida?

Clearly cotton was king in all the inhabited land of northern Florida during the antebellum days. With the end of the Civil War, many planters in the north of the state continued a while with cotton but began to diversify, trying cash crops like vegetables and fruit.

49. How and when did Florida's cattle raising begin?

It began in 1521 with the arrival of the first Spaniards who brought cattle from southern Spain. Much of Florida's ranching today is in the Kissimmee area.

50. What is the most important mining industry in Florida?

The state's most important mining industry is phosphate. Four-fifths of the nation's phosphate comes from Florida. The state supplies a quarter of the world's need.

51. What are the negative aspects of mining phosphate?

The industry is criticized for polluting the air, water and soil. There were instances where cattle and citrus growing became impossible in certain areas. Fish had been known to die in water near phosphate yields.

52. Who introduced the orange to Florida?

The Spanish brought the orange with them when they settled St. Augustine. The orange seeds came from southern Spain where winters are mild and oranges grow all year.

53. How important is citrus growing to Florida's overall economy?

Citrus growing is Florida's most important agricultural industry. Florida produces about 75% of the nation's oranges, grapefruits, lemons and limes. The orange blossom is Florida's state flower.

54. How many farm workers are needed in the fields and orchards of Florida on a continuous basis?

Although the numbers vary, about eighty-five thousand workers are needed to work the fields and orchards. These workers come mostly from Central or South America or Vietnam.

55. What happened to the convict lease program that supplied convict labor for farm use in the past?

This practice was discontinued in 1922, because of the brutal treatment of prisoners, especially in the turpentine camps.

The Wildlife

56. What are some of the animals that lived in Florida thousands of years ago but are now extinct?

There is evidence that Florida was once the home of the woolly mammoth, the mastodon and the giant tree sloth.

57. Where have archeologists found evidence of the mammoth in the state?

Recently archeologists have discovered a mammoth's skeleton on the Peace River in Central Florida. Boy scouts had found a tusk protruding from the mud in the riverbank.

58. What has been the nemesis of the Florida panther?

For three centuries, the Florida panther has been persecuted by white Floridians out of fear. The Indians were wise in leaving this magnificent animal alone. There is no record of any attack by a panther on a human being in Florida.

59. Why does the panther still face extinction?

This reclusive animal faces extinction—not because of the Indian ceremonies involving it but because of the freeways and large housing developments, which have obliterated its natural habitat. The panther lives primarily in the Everglades.

60. How did the alligator get its name?

The early Spaniards called this reptile "el largarto." Alligator is a corruption by the English of the Spanish name.

61. Has the alligator population of Florida suffered over the years?

The Florida alligator almost disappeared at the turn of the century. Laws now prevent hunting alligators for their skins. The population has again risen to about one million in the state. Now, occasional alligator hunting is allowed.

62. Are alligators dangerous only in the water?

Most alligator attacks occur in the water, often when an unsuspecting animal has gone into a river to drink. Alligators occasionally attack on dry land and have been known to run up to 28 miles an hour.

63. Is the armadillo a native of Florida?

Armadillos migrated from Texas. They have hard shells in their backs and long snouts for digging. They are not dangerous to humans but can be a nuisance to lawns and vegetable gardens. This is the only mammal besides humans that can contract leprosy.

64. In Florida, what is known as "The Gentle Giant?"

The Gentle Giant is the West Indian manatee. This creature is threatened by development and has begun to disappear. There may be at present only about 3000 manatees in the waters of Florida.

65. Why are the manatees starting to disappear?

Their natural habitat is threatened by drainage and development. They are large animals, weighing sometimes as much as 3,500 pounds. They often cannot get out of the way of motorboats that often injure them with their propellers.

66. What are the most dangerous snakes in the state?

There are many kinds of snakes in Florida but the poisonous ones are: the coral snake, certain rattlesnakes, and the cottonmouth, which is also called the water moccasin.

67. What are the most common wading birds in the Everglades?

The long-legged shore birds are the great egret, the snowy egret and the roseate spoonbill.

68. What has been done to protect the extinction of exotic birds from hunters?

Three dates mark a progressive concern to protect birds from hunters. In 1916, a small area of the Everglades was set aside. This became the Royal Palm State Park. In 1931, Congress of the United States passed a bill to protect most of South Florida's wildlife. In 1947, President Truman dedicated the Everglades National Park.

69. Which birds in the Everglades are diving and underwater swimmers?

The diving and underwater swimmers are the anhinga and the wood stork.

70. Why is the Florida anhinga also called the "snake bird?"

As the anhinga fishes for its food, it swims under water with only its head and neck above water. It looks like a snake as it travels across the water. Before it can fly again, the anhinga must dry out its wings.

71. Why was Guy Bradley shot to death?

The Audubon Society was concerned about the needless killing of birds in the Everglades and hired Bradley to study the problem and report to them. Birds were being shot for their feathers. On

July 8th, 1905, Bradley was found dead in his skiff. Game violators were suspected of this killing but there was insufficient evidence. After another killing, a law was passed banning the use of feathers on hats, which helped to reduce the shooting of birds.

72. What are the types of herons found throughout the state?

These wading birds can be found near bodies of water. The two types that are most easily recognizable are the great blue and the great white heron. The flamingo is a member of this family.

73. Where are most of the sea turtles in Florida?

They make their habitat in the tropical waters around the Everglades. There are five species whose numbers have diminished by hunters and development.

74. How long is the nesting season for Florida's sea turtles?

The season lasts from May through October. Females, weighing between one hundred and four hundred pounds, drop about one hundred eggs in a hole they dig on the beach, cover the eggs and head back to sea. About one in a thousand baby turtles may reach maturity.

75. Is it true that Florida has the only turtle hospital in the United States?

Yes. On Marathon Key, there is the Hidden Harbor Turtle Hospital, which came into being because of the growing tendency for turtles to develop tumors.

76. Why is the harvesting of oysters so important to Apalachicola?

About 90% of the oysters in Florida come from Apalachicola. These oysters thrive because the fresh water from the Apalachicola River is rich in nutrients.

77. Why are oysters best when eaten between December and March or during the "R" months?

During the warmer months, more sweet water is mixed with the seawater. This creates conditions for marine microorganisms like vibrio vulnificus to grow in the oysters. For most people, this is not dangerous.

78. Are jellyfish, found along the Florida coast, dangerous?

They are not dangerous but their sting can cause considerable pain. The protein in the venom causes this discomfort. One should be careful where one swims or walks along the beaches.

79. How many varieties of shells have been categorized from the beaches of Florida?

More than fifteen hundred varieties of shells have been noted. Storms have a tendency of stirring up shells and depositing them along the shore.

80. Where did sponge gathering have its origin in the state?

The industry had its start in the Florida Keys in the 1850s but reached the Tampa Bay area about fifty years later.

81. What is the sponge made of?

The sponge is an aquatic creature that lives at the sea bottom. The sponge is in reality a colony of millions of one-cell organisms that are bound together.

Native People

82. How far back in time have native people lived in Florida?

Conservative estimates are that The Arawak tribes from the West Indies in the Caribbean came to Florida about ten thousand years ago.

83. What generic name do we give to these early Floridians?

We refer to them as Paleo-Indian. They were hunters and gatherers but had no noticeable skills with clay.

84. Is there any alternative view of the origin of the early natives of Florida?

Some believe that the first residents of Florida were descended from Eurasians who crossed the ice bridge from Siberia to Alaska. There is little evidence that either theory is correct.

85. At what point did the early native Floridians begin making pottery?

Through archeological digs, it has been determined that these natives began making pottery by 2000 B.C. This is almost eight hundred years before any other Native American. These natives seemed to know how to fire clay objects for their daily use like pots and water vessels.

86. What Indian tribes lived in Florida at the time of the arrival of the Spaniards?

These natives were called the Calusa. They were builders of sacred dwellings or flat-topped mounds. They relied almost exclusively on the sea for food.

87. What do we know about Florida's pre-Columbian culture in the area of Tallahassee and Leon County?

Archaeologists have named the development The Fort Walton Culture. It was noted for its settled villages, stores of food and population growth and, again, the high earthen mounds.

88. By what name were these natives known?

The natives that the Spaniards encountered in the Tallahassee area were the Apalachee.

89. Is there any evidence as to how the natives viewed death in their culture?

From artifacts, it is believed that the natives viewed death as a voyage to another world. For this journey, the dead warriors, for example, were given weapons for hunting, tools for building and food for sustenance.

90. What do we understand was the religious beliefs of the early natives?

Similar to other early peoples, the Floridian natives worshipped everything they could not understand—the sun, the sea, the storm and familiar animals.

91. What were the crops planted by the native people of Florida?

Prior to the arrival of the Spaniards, the natives planted corn, beans, squash, including the pumpkin.

92. Who were the original inhabitants of the Everglades?

They were referred to as "The People of the Glade." They lived in permanent villages and built canoes for hunting and fishing. The Spaniards reduced the numbers of these natives through fighting, disease and slavery. By 1800, only a small community of these natives remained.

93. After the departure of the Spanish from southern Florida, what tribe came to replace the People of the Glade?

The Muskogee Creek People moved south from areas that are now the Carolinas, Georgia and Alabama. They later became know as "Seminole."

94. How did the natives react to the arrival of Spaniards to their land?

First they reacted with curiosity and fear. They quickly learned that they had to obey the invaders because the foreigners possessed a superior means of warfare.

95. What did the natives seem to fear most in their contact with the Spaniards?

They feared the horses, which they had never seen before and they feared the guns that seemed to explode in their faces.

96. What were the natives called who occupied the Miami area?

The Tequesta Indian lived in this area before the arrival of the Spaniards. They used their canoes to travel along the coast to trade with other tribes.

97. What other native populations lived in Florida in the 1500s?

In addition to the Apalachee who lived in the northwest and the

Tequesta and Calusa tribes on the southern coasts, there were the Ais who occupied the central Atlantic Coast and the Timucuans who occupied the northeast regions. On the gulf coast, near present-day Tampa were the Tocobaga.

98. Is the name of the capital Tallahassee of Indian origin?

It is believed that "Tallahassee" was translated from the Creek language. "Talwa" meaning "town" and "Ahassee" meaning "old"—therefore Tallahassee was Creek for Old Town. It is also said that on December 11th, 1824, the lawmakers officially named the village "Tallahassee" because the acting governor of West Florida—George Walton's fourteen-year-old daughter, Octavia, suggested the name to them.

99. How did the Native Americans leave their mark in what is known today as Oskaloosa County?

Between 1200 and 1700 A.D., Native Americans built a ceremonial mound of over a hundred thousand cubic feet of soil and seashells.

100. When did the Creek Indians settle in Florida?

The Creek Indians left Georgia to settle in Florida in 1750. They became known later as the Seminoles.

101. How was it that the Upper and Lower Creek Indians, known for warring with each other, lived in comparative harmony when they settled in Florida?

These warring factions of the Creek Nation found abundant living space, many deer and a considerable number of wild cattle that had come from the abandoned Spanish ranches.

102. What was the official US version for the reasons that started the First Seminole War?

In the U.S. version of events, the Seminole Indians attacked a boat carrying American troops on the Apalachicola River.

103. What may have been the real reason for the beginning of the First Seminole War?

General Andrew Jackson wanted the land that the Seminole Indians had in East Florida and decided to chase them out. Besides, the Indians were protecting runaway slaves that had to be returned to their owners. The year was 1817.

104. In what way did the Creek and Seminole Indians come into contact with the black fugitive slaves?

Often the slaves would escape from Carolina, Georgia and Alabama and seek refuge among the Indians in the forests of north Florida.

105. How were the fugitive slaves useful to the Indian communities?

The slaves often spoke English and could serve as translators for the Indians.

106. In what way did the Seminole and Creek communities differ in regards to the slaves?

The Seminoles freely intermarried with the blacks while the conservative Creeks did not.

107. Did the Creek Indians precede the Seminoles in settling in Florida?

No. The Seminoles preceded the Creeks by about fifty years. The first Seminoles probably came after Queen Anne's War, which ended in 1713.

108. How did General Jackson further justify his actions against the Seminoles?

He accused the Indians of a series of incursions against US property. On this occasion, he used his Tennessee troops to drive out the Indians and take the Spanish fort of St. Marks. Jackson then went west to Pensacola and demanded the Spanish surrender their possessions there.

109. How did the Second Seminole War begin?

To encourage population growth and more white settlers coming to Florida, the US government offered to move the Seminole Indians to Oklahoma. Some moved willingly, not wanting to fight against the army of the United States. Some defied the order.

110. Who was the leader of the Seminoles that defied the US Government's order to leave Florida?

The leader was Osceola. He and his followers fled south into the Everglades and fought against the US forces for seven years.

111. How did General Thomas Jessup use less than legal tactics to capture Osceola?

Jessup invited Osceola to talks under a flag of truce. He then took the leader into custody with his immediate family. The year was 1842. General Jessup was severely criticized for this breach in behavior. Osceola was put into prison and died there.

112. What is the meaning of the French expression "bras coupé?"

It means, "arm cut off" and refers to a man without freedom—a man with his arm cut off. This is an Indian legend, which later was written out by George Washington Cable. The story became an opera by Frederick Delius, "Koanga," and premiered in America in 1970.

113. Who led the Seminole Indians in their last wars against the white man?

Billy Bowlegs was the leader and caused considerable grief to the white settlers until Governor Broome concentrated his efforts to find the hiding place of this chief. After two years, Bowlegs' camp was found and he surrendered. The year was 1858.

114. How many American Indians are living in Florida today?

Exact numbers are not certain. It is believed that those who have not integrated with the white communities are about 3000.

115. Are these Indians the Seminoles?

Again, numbers are deceiving but it is believed that 2500 are Seminoles and about 500 hundred are Miccosukee Indians. About twenty-five miles west of Miami is a Miccosukee village. They are descendants from those natives who avoided deportation during the Indian wars.

116. Where does the name "Seminole" come from?

The word probably derived from "siminoli" which means exiles or wanderers.

The Spaniards

117. Before the arrival of the Spaniards on the coast of Florida, is it possible that Americus Vespucci may have touched the coast of Florida on his voyage in 1497?

It is possible but of his travels he speaks about sailing around the Peninsula of Yucatan and visiting Little Venice (Venezuela) and then on to Tampico, following the Gulf and passing the mouth of the Mississippi. It is possible that he sailed right by Florida on his way to the Chesapeake Bay.

118. Would the voyage of Sebastian Cabot to the Atlantic shore of America in 1497 have included a trip to Florida?

It is not likely. His log contains descriptions of the northern latitudes and it is doubtful he would have gone as far south as Florida.

119. Who then is credited with the discovery (for Europeans) of Florida?

Juan Ponce de Leon is generally credited with being the discoverer of Florida. He left Puerto Rico on March 3, 1513, leading an expedition in search of the fabled waters with rejuvenating powers. He landed on or near the point we call today Melbourne Beach on April 2nd.

120. How did Florida get its name?

Juan Ponce de Leon called the land " La Florida" which meant "flowery land." The countryside was covered with beautiful flowers that spring.

121. Did Ponce de Leon establish a colony in Florida in 1513?

No. There were several factors, which prevented him from staying. The hostility of the natives was very intense; this was the main reason.

122. Aside from the positive motivations for wanting to explore the coast of Florida in the 1500s, what were the negative factors?

Aside from the hostility of the natives, the Straits of Florida were treacherous and stormy certain times of the year. The seas were often rough, hiding dangerous reefs. The narrow straits terrified the navigators.

123. What was the King of Spain's reason for having Ponce de Leon go to Florida?

Ponce de Leon's commission was not to explore Florida, which at the time was unknown to the Spanish king, but to conquer the land called the "Island of Bimini." The king's motivation was, as it had been since Columbus' first voyage, to find precious metals and stones.

124. How was Ponce de Leon so familiar with the "New World?"

He had accompanied Christopher Columbus on his second voyage to the Americas. Ponce de Leon remained and became the governor of Puerto Rico. Although Ponce de Leon is given credit for discovering Florida, Spain's trade records show that Spanish ships, probably slavers, stopped on the southwest end of the peninsula as early as 1510.

125. What irony was there in Ponce de Leon's quest for eternal life in the Fountain of Youth?

Instead of finding extended life, he found a quick death on his second trip to Florida at the hands of the Indians.

126. Who were the Spanish explorers to follow Ponce de Leon?

The first non-permanent colony was established during the third voyage of Lucas Vasquez de Ayllon in 1526. This was the first white colony within the present United States. Although it was Ponce de Leon who claimed Florida for King Ferdinand V of Spain, it was Panfilo de Narvaez who landed with several hundred men in Florida and began to explore the land. This was near Tampa Bay in the year of 1528.

127. What do we know about Hernando de Soto's exploration of Florida?

In May of 1539, he landed in Tampa Bay with about six hundred men. His mission was to find gold. His journal speaks of his passing through the areas known today as Dade City, Gainesville, Lake City and Tallahassee.

128. What had Hernando de Soto accomplished before sailing to Florida?

He had been one of the twelve conquerors of Peru. This venture had made him very rich and he was eager to explore Florida for whatever riches he could find.

129. What is the legacy of the De Soto period?

Unfortunately it is not good. He was obsessed by his desire for gold and the fame it would bring him. He was needlessly cruel to the natives and made no attempt at understanding them. Many natives died as a result of the contagious diseases the Spaniards left in their wake.

130. How did the Spanish explorers justify their cruelty to the natives?

They believed that these Indians had no souls; that they, like animals, were placed on earth to serve Christians.

131. How long did De Soto remain in Tallahassee?

He spent the winter of 1539–40 near the present-day capitol, according to artifacts found in 1987. He may very well have been the first person to celebrate mass in Florida on Christmas Day. It was in a location known today as Lake Jackson.

132. Who wrote the first book about Florida?

Records show that Escalante de Fonteneda was shipwrecked in 1545. He wrote the first book about Florida after spending seventeen years living among the natives.

133. How did the early Spaniards understand the geography of the New World?

They had no concept of real distances but understood them in terms of their own frame of reference—the distances in their homeland. De Soto, for example, thought the silver mines of Zacateca, Mexico were only a day's journey from Florida.

134. When was the Pensacola area first explored?

In 1558, Philip II of Spain authorized the Viceroy of New Spain, Luis de Velasco, to lead an expedition with 1500 soldiers and settlers. He landed in Pensacola but found the land unsuitable and the natives hostile. From 1559–1561, Tristan de Luna tried to establish a foothold here but was unsuccessful.

135. From available records, what were the wild animals that the early Spaniards found in Florida?

They found lions, bears, wolves, deer, jackals and rabbits. The wild fowl consisted of cranes, ducks, pigeons, thrushes and sparrows. They found other wildlife for which they had no names.

136. What had the early Spaniards found of food sources growing naturally or in cultivation?

They noted that the natives had bread, which was made exclusively from maize. Fruit was very common. There were persimmons, mulberries, grapes and walnuts. The local Indians ate a fruit from a plant similar to the pear.

137. When was the first permanent Spanish settlement established in Florida?

The first permanent settlement was established at St. Augustine in 1565. Its founder was Pedro Menendez de Aviles. He arrived under orders from Philip II of Spain on the feast day of St. Augustine. This is how the settlement got its name.

138. Did the settlement of St. Augustine precede the settlements of Jamestown and Plymouth Rock?

Yes. St. Augustine was settled in 1565. The English settled Jamestown in 1607 and Plymouth Rock in 1620.

139. How long did it take the Spanish clergy to establish missions in Florida?

While the civil authorities were seeking gold, the Franciscan friars were eager to win souls for the Catholic Church. After the establishment of St Augustine, nine friars, with the help of natives, began, in 1573, to construct their missions. By 1615, the Spaniards had constructed more than twenty missions in the areas we know today as Florida, Georgia and South Carolina.

140. What were the purposes of these missions?

They were places where the natives could live, work and learn about Christianity. The natives were baptized in order to save their souls from damnation. The Franciscans were eager to teach the natives about the plants they had brought with them from Spain.

141. Was Spain the only country interested in establishing settlements in Florida?

No. In 1564, a French expedition established a colony named Fort Caroline near the mouth of the St. Johns River, that the French named Rivière de Mai.

142. What did the Spanish learn from the natives' use of nut grass?

The roots of the nut grass were dried and crushed into powder. The Indians rubbed it into their bodies to refresh the skin or they took it internally with water to cure stomach distress.

143. In what way was the Spanish occupation of Florida and New Mexico similar?

Both began with the purpose of discovering large quantities of gold. Neither Florida nor New Mexico yielded the treasures the Spanish sought.

144. How linguistically does Florida differ from New Mexico?

The Spanish language influence was strong in New Mexico; whereas, due to the French and English influence, the Spanish language, until recently, did not play a continued role in Florida.

145. Why was the expedition by France to the shores of Florida in 1562 kept a secret from Spain?

The French expedition commanded by Jean Ribaut of Dieppe, France had tacit approval of the King of France but it was kept a secret because the French were planning to settle in a territory claimed by Spain. With a crew of 150 men, Jean Ribaut crossed the Atlantic in two and a half months, landing just north of St. Augustine.

146. What was the purpose of the French colony and how did the French propose to avoid Spanish intervention?

The French established a Huguenot colony, for the purpose of expressing religious freedom in the New World. To avoid Spanish intervention, the French claimed that they were a private venture only and did not come representing the King of France.

147. Did the Spanish accept this reason?

They found this excuse ludicrous, since leading the French expedition was the famous French Admiral Coligny, who had come to Florida at the behest of the Queen of France. When Spain protested to Charles IX that France had encroached on its territory, France responded that it made a distinction between "lands conquered" and "lands occupied." Since the Spanish had not occupied the area of the Huguenot colony, it was fair game to be occupied by others.

148. How did the Spanish respond to this?

Philip II of Spain sent Pedro Menéndez de Avilés to destroy the French colony and massacre its occupants. Fort Caroline was completely destroyed. The year was 1565.

149. What made Philip II such a formidable power in Europe at the time?

Not only was he a brilliant and feared monarch in his own right; but also he was the son of Charles V—sovereign of Spain, of the Netherlands, of Naples, of part of central Italy, and of Navarre. Philip II inherited his father's drive, vision and strength. After the massacre of the Huguenots, Philip II justified this action by calling the occupants of Fort Caroline heretics, who did not believe in the true Church. In a letter to the Queen of France, Catherine de Medici, Philip II wrote "... I have given orders to chastise them [your subjects] as thieving pirates."

150. Did France take revenge for this terrible massacre?

Not officially, but a private adventurer, Dominic de Gourges, took it upon himself to attack the Spanish at their settlement on the St. Johns River and kill as many Spaniards as he could. Neither the French nor the Spanish reported this incident but the Huguenots did.

151. What did France do when the Spanish chased them from Florida?

They concentrated their efforts around the Mississippi River and built their colonies there.

152. What initially brought France and England to the New World?

On one hand the Protestant groups were seeking religious freedom but perhaps, more importantly, they had seen the great wealth Spain had acquired in Central and South America and wanted to find similar wealth.

153. What action did England take against the Spaniards in Florida in 1586?

In 1586, Sir Francis Drake attacked, looted and burned St. Augustine in a hit-and-run action.

154. What did the British do to cause continued concern to the Spanish in the sixteen hundreds?

Having driven the French out of Fort Caroline, the Spanish then saw that the British had successfully settled in Jamestown, Virginia in 1607 and Charleston, South Carolina in 1670.

155. When were Spain's missions established in the Apalachicola area?

Franciscan friars settled in this area in 1655. Apalachicola, in the language of the natives means, "land beyond." As many as 40,000 natives lived along this coast at the time of the Spaniards' arrival.

156. Had the Jesuits played no role in the establishment of missions in Florida?

The priests that accompanied Menendez de Aviles to St. Augustine were Jesuits but they withdrew in 1572.

157. How did the Spanish seek to protect themselves from the British who had settled to the north of the St. Johns River?

The Spanish built the Castillo de San Marcos, which was completed in 1695 in St. Augustine. It remains the oldest masonry fort in the United States.

158. What may have been the most disputed area in the entire United States?

Amelia Island, named in honor of Princess Amelia, daughter of George II, existed from the mid-fifteen hundreds through the late eighteen hundreds under eight different flags—French, Spanish, English, Patriots, Green Cross of Florida, Mexican Rebel, Confederate and American.

159. What problems was Spain experiencing at home during the seventeen hundreds?

The colonies in America were proving too costly for Spain. Wars in Europe were depleting its treasuries. Spain's far-flung empire required more and more support, without the hope of the riches it had hoped for. The Catholic Church insisted that the king could not abandon all the newly baptized natives for fear of losing their immortal souls.

160. What financial disaster did Spain suffer as a result of a storm along the Atlantic coast in 1715?

A fleet of Spanish ships sank in a terrible storm at Sebastian Inlet that year. The galleons were loaded with gold and silver.

161. How did the British keep the Spanish off balance in the early years of the seventeen hundreds?

Carolina Governor James Moore organized an attack on St. Augustine in 1702. Although the Spanish drove him off, it was the start of several battles. Two years later, Moore led another military attack on the missions. By 1708, the missions of Apalachee were taken and destroyed.

162. How did Americans differ from the European powers in their quest for land?

The British and the Spanish left the Indians in undisturbed possession of most of the interior. The Americans could hardly tolerate their presence anywhere.

163. How did Spain lose Cuba and regain it again?

When France began moving its fur trading east from the Mississippi and England began moving west from the Atlantic, a war broke out in which Spain sided with France. This is what we call the "French and Indian War." At war's end, England had captured Cuba from Spain. In 1763, Spain traded its possessions in Florida in exchange for Cuba.

164. What secret accord between France and Spain was designed to hurt England's interests?

Before the conclusion of the war in 1763, France secretly transferred Louisiana to Spain to save it from British control.

165. How did the treaty at the end of the French and Indian War (Called the Seven Years' War in Europe) affect Florida?

The treaty restored the Philippines and Cuba to Spain but gave all of Florida to England.

166. How did the British seek to populate Florida when they took control in 1763?

The British issued more that 280 large land grants in East and West Florida during this period.

167. How long did Florida remain under British control?

England retained control of Florida for twenty years.

168. What is meant by the Bourbon Era?

During the period of the Reconstruction, the democrats were called Bourbons, in reference to the French Bourbons, which meant they had learned nothing and forgotten nothing. It was meant to be a derogatory reference.

169. How did the American Revolution affect England's control over Florida?

While Great Britain was occupied fighting the thirteen colonies, Spain invaded West Florida. In 1781, Great Britain ceded West Florida to Spain. Two years later, Spain took Pensacola and East Florida from England as well.

170. What was the best-known event of Spain's participation in the American Revolution?

The best-known event of Spain's participation was the siege by Bernando Galvez against the British at Pensacola.

171. Were there as many stars in the American Flag in 1776 as colonies?

There were thirteen stars in the American flag. There were, however, seventeen original colonies. Upper and Lower Canada were two colonies in the north and East and West Florida in the south.

172. During the twenty years of British control of Florida, how did the Catholic Church fare?

During this period, the Catholic Church lost most of its communicants and several Protestant denominations got their start in Florida. Their numbers grew quickly throughout the region.

173. Why was Spain's second foothold in Florida so tenuous?

First of all, Spain was less powerful in 1783 than it had been in the sixteen hundreds. Additionally, Spain had to contend with English-speaking settlers from the north, which became more numerous than the Spanish-speaking inhabitants. Finally, there was the constant concern that American expansion would eventually take all of Florida.

174. About the time that Mexico was declaring its independence from Spain, what was happening in Florida?

In 1819, the United States signed a treaty with Spain, which formally ceded all of Florida to the States. By 1821, Florida had become a territory of the US. The terms of the treaty gave the US the responsibility of assuming five million dollars worth of debt the Spanish had with American citizens and required the US to surrender any claims it had to Texas.

175. When did the US Government acquire Key West?

Spain turned Key West over to the US in 1821 along with the rest of Florida. The Spanish had named Key West "Cayo Hueso" or Bone Key.

176. What was the name of the treaty by which Florida became a territory of the United States?

The treaty was called the Adams-Onis Treaty. It was signed in 1819. Three years later, President James Monroe signed a law establishing the territory of Florida. This joined East and West Florida.

177. How many years had Spain been in possession of territory in the New World?

Spain's presence in the New World began with Christopher Columbus in 1492 and ended with Spain's losing Cuba in 1898. Spanish dominion in the New World would last for more than four centuries. During that time, thousands of churches were built, presiding over thousands of plazas, affecting the faith, language and culture of millions of people.

Events and People of the 1800s and Before

178. Who was responsible for the burning of St. Augustine in 1705?

In 1705, British forces attacked Florida, destroying Spanish missions in the north and burning most of St. Augustine.

179. What were the results of the British attack on St. Augustine?

Under the command of British Governor James Moore, the British troops were trapped in the harbor of St. Augustine. Spanish ships sent from Cuba blocked the British and forced them to make their retreat overland. Moore later got his revenge on the Spanish by having his men, with the help of the Indians, destroy the chain of Spanish missions.

180. At what moment in history was the first periodical published in Florida?

It was the *East Florida Gazette* established in St. Augustine in 1783. Florida has now more than 250 newspapers.

181. Why weren't the inhabitants of Florida concerned about the election of George Washington, the first President of the United States?

Floridians, in 1789, celebrated the new King of Spain—their king, Charles IV. Florida had not yet become a territory of the U.S.

182. How did the sale of the Louisiana region affect Florida?

President Thomas Jefferson bought the large tract of land between Florida and Texas from the French in 1803. This was known as the Louisiana Purchase. This drove a wedge between the two great Spanish possessions on the North American Continent.

183. When did the United States formally halt the trade of slaves from Africa?

In 1808, the US formally halted slave trade with Africa but more than 200,000 more slaves entered the US between that date and the Civil War. Many of these slaves came by way of Cuba where this trade was still legal.

184. What suggestion brought the idea of the establishment of a bank in Florida?

Military Governor Andrew Jackson wanted to establish a branch of the United States Bank in Pensacola in 1821. Although the idea was planted in the minds of the inhabitants, the territorial legislature rejected the idea.

185. What event commemorated the first real newspaper in Florida?

Just as Florida became a territory in 1821, the first newspaper was published in St. Augustine. It was the *Florida Gazette*.

186. Which early Florida governor was made famous by an American author?

The famous American writer, Washington Irving depicted William Duval, the first Territorial Governor of Florida, as a hero model.

187. What event commemorates the landing of Spanish explorers on the shores of Florida?

At the De Soto National Memorial in Bradenton (forty-nine miles south of Tampa), citizens dress up in 16th century costumes to commemorate the landing of De Soto in Florida.

188. Under what circumstances did electricity come to Florida?

Florida became Thomas Edison's adopted state. Because of his poor health, he moved to Ft. Myers and bought thirteen acres. When he offered to provide the city with free electricity, the community declined for fear the cows would be disturbed by the light. He later made the St. James Hotel in Jacksonville the first location in Florida to have his new invention—light.

189. What famous author moved south to Florida from Boston in 1827, for reasons of his health?

Ralph Waldo Emerson had a lung condition, which was made worse by the cold, damp weather of Boston. He moved to St. Augustine for a while but did not stay.

190. What was the occasion that gave the USS Constitution its nickname "Old Ironsides?"

In 1828, President John Quincy Adams set aside 1,400 acres for Santa Rosa Live Oak Timber Reservation. It was excellent oak for sea vessels. The wood was called "ironwood" for its density. Thus the USS Constitution built of this wood got its nickname.

191. What Pensacola businessman created his own bank to house the money the government had sent him?

William Chase started his own bank for his brick-making business in 1830. He then started a railway to carry his supplies.

192. What is the event known as the "Dade Massacre?"

In 1835, the Seminole Indians ambushed Major Francis Dade and more that one hundred of his men. All were killed but three. This event led to seven years of bloody conflict.

193. What main event brought about the depression in Florida after the Second Seminole War?

The event that triggered this depression was the failure of the Union Bank of Tallahassee in 1837.

194. How did the yellow fever epidemic of 1841 get its start?

Two infected men from Havana, Cuba came ashore in Florida at St. Joseph. From there the disease spread to Tallahassee.

195. What were possible causes for the great Tallahassee fire of 1843?

Drought conditions existed throughout the city and surrounding area. The fire started on May 25th in the late afternoon and consumed most of the downtown area. No firefighting equipment was available to help limit the destruction.

196. What were the main causes for the failure of Union Bank and its closure in 1843?

There were several reasons for the failure of the Union Bank. There was poor administration; a nation-wide depression brought about by President Jackson's fiscal policies and money borrowed against faith bonds.

197. When did Florida become a state in the United States?

On March 3rd 1845, Florida became the twenty-seventh state in the Union. It entered as a slave state. Congress passed the bill and President John Tyler signed it into law.

198. How did Christmas, Florida get its name?

During the Seminole Wars, soldiers stopped here, 25 miles east of Orlando, to build a fort. Since it was the Christmas Season, the builders named their settlement after the holiday.

199. What is the principal controversy connected with the Annual Springtime Tallahassee Festival?

This festival recognizes that Andrew Jackson was an important and colorful figure in Florida history. Native Americans and African Americans protest Jackson's vicious brutality against their people.

200. What were the events that led Florida towards secession?

There were several events, such as the birth of the Republican Party, The Dred Scott Decision, John Brown's raid on Harper's Ferry, the publication of *Uncle Tom's Cabin*, and finally Lincoln's victory in 1860. All these events filled Floridians with fear and a desire to secede from the Union.

201. What was the basic purpose of the Homestead Act of 1866?

It was designed to give freedmen and loyal whites a chance for owning land. New settlers to Florida were given 160-acre parcels. They would be required to live on the land and farm it for five years before they could own it.

202. Who was the first black to be elected to the Congress of the United States?

John Willis Menard was the first black to be elected to this body. However, Congress refused him admission. In 1873, he won a seat in the Florida House of Representatives.

203. What were the results of the election of 1876?

The results marked the end of the Republican Congressional Reconstruction and the return of control to white democrats in Florida.

204. Who invented the basic technology for air conditioning and refrigeration?

A Floridian doctor by the name of John Gorrie had the basic idea for air conditioning. He managed to get a patent for his work in 1880. It wasn't until a hundred years later that this technology became widespread.

205. When did Florida's railroads begin their extension?

The real extension of railroads began in the 1880s, although a few hundred miles of track existed during the Civil War. Today there are more than 6,500 miles of track.

206. What great Florida land purchase was Hamilton Disston remembered for?

In 1881, Hamilton Disston from Pennsylvania bought 4 million acres of Central Florida. He paid about twenty-five cents an acre. Today part of that property is home to Walt Disney World.

207. How did the theory of white supremacy affect the law?

By 1887, a series of Jim Crow laws were enacted to further subjugate the blacks.

208. What was the effect of "Lynch laws" on blacks?

Lynch laws were specifically designed to keep blacks in "their place." Between 1889 and 1918, there were 160 instances of lynching of blacks in Florida.

209. What were some of the restrictions of the Jim Crow" laws?

They were mostly measures of segregation in public transportation, restaurants, theaters, parks and restrooms.

210. What economic interests did the US have in Cuba in the 1890s?

Florida had strong ties to Cuba. More than 50 million dollars were invested in Cuba and more than 100 thousand dollars came in trade each year to the US, mostly from Cuban tobacco and raw sugar.

211. What fears did Florida have as the US was preparing for war against Spain over Cuban independence?

Florida feared that Cuba might be annexed to the US and become an even greater competitor in the production of fruit, vegetables and tobacco. Floridians also feared the competition in tourism.

212. How did the declaration of war with Spain solve the problems of rivalry with Cuba?

With the declaration of war in April 1898 came the Teller Amendment, which forswore any annexation of Cuba to the United States.

213. How did landowner Julia D. Tuttle convince Henry Flagler that the destructive freeze of 1894–95 had not reached Miami?

She sent him an orange blossom packaged in cotton. Subsequently, she deeded her land north of the Miami River to Flagler.

214. Who was the British pirate to lead the Creek Indians against the French and Spanish in a fur trade dispute in 1802?

It was William Augustus Bowles. He was shipwrecked after attacking the fort at St. Marks and thrown into a Cuban dungeon where he died.

215. When the Marquis de Lafayette was urged to settle in Florida, what was his response?

It was Richard Keith Call who offered Lafayette a congressional grant of land comprised of thirty-six square miles. Lafayette, however, refused to settle in Florida because he was an abolitionist. He did, however, accept the land and established a free colony.

216. Who were the "Crackers?"

There is controversy as to the origin of the term. Old time cattle drivers ran great herds of cattle across Florida to shipping points, popping long cowhide whips so loudly that they could be heard miles away. The cracking sound gave these men their nicknames.

217. What northern inventor made his laboratory in Ft. Myers so he could spend his winters in Florida?

Thomas Edison experimented with several of his ideas. In Florida he experimented with rubber. He also planted more than 500 species of plants.

218. Which early governor had the most impressive background for office?

John Branch, the sixth territorial governor (1844–45), had previously been a US Senator of North Carolina and served as Andrew Jackson's Secretary of the Navy.

219. How many governors has Florida had since the state was admitted to the Union in 1845?

There have been 41 governors of Florida since 1845, beginning with William D. Moseley.

220. Who was Andrew Turnbull?

Dr. Andrew Turnbull received a land grant in Florida but unlike many such grantees, he took advantage of the land to bring 1400 workers from Menorca, Greece and Italy to work as indentured servants. Turnbull founded the indigo-producing colony of New Smyrna.

221. Who was Tallahassee's most noted antebellum physician?

It was Dr. Edward Bradford who was a native of North Carolina. He came to Leon County in 1831 to practice medicine and manage his own plantation. He bought 3,200 acres of land ten miles from the capital.

222. Who were the new immigrants that came to Florida in 1845?

Many were the very poor from the Appalachian Mountains who came to Florida looking for work. That year, the population of Florida climbed to fifty-eight thousand.

223. Why is the name Hamilton Disston important in Florida history?

Disston was an important industrialist and developer. He purchased 4 million acres in central Florida in 1881 for development purposes.

224. What was General Andrew Jackson's role during the War of 1812?

He marched into Pensacola—a Spanish territory but inhabited by the British. He drove the British out and then went on the New Orleans to take it away from the British as well.

225. What was the principal motivation of the War of 1812?

James Madison wanted to drive the British out of Florida, which Great Britain had been using for supply purposes. Andrew Jackson marched into Pensacola and captured it in 1813.

226. What was the reason for Andrew Jackson's third trip to Florida?

He came to Florida for the third time to receive the post as the first military governor of Florida—the new US territory. He resigned three months later to return to Tennessee.

227. What pretext did General Jackson use in 1813, to move his troops across the border into Florida?

The Creek Indians attacked several hundred settlers at Fort Mims. This Alabama raid gave General Jackson the pretext he needed to attack both Indians and British in Pensacola.

228. What legacy did Andrew Jackson leave to Florida before he returned to Tennessee?

He began the Americanization of Florida; he established trial by jury and established county courts.

229. How did Zachary Taylor make his reputation before becoming President of the United States?

Zachary Taylor commanded American forces during the Second Seminole War. Ten years after the war, in 1850, he became the twelfth US President.

230. Who was the famous nephew of Napoleon to settle in Florida?

It was Prince Achille Murat. He was the nephew, through marriage, to Napoleon. Murat married Catherine Daingerfield Willis Gray who was the great-grandniece of George Washington.

231.What brought Harriet Beecher Stowe to live in Florida?

Her son, Fred, had been injured during the Civil War at Gettysburg and decided to move to Florida. Stowe came to visit her son and decided to build a cottage to spend her winters there.

232. Who was the first person to introduce sponge gathering to Tarpin Springs?

Although sponge gathering began in the Florida Keys around 1850, George Cocoris, a Greek, introduced this industry to Tarpin Springs in 1905. He had the first underwater apparatus—helmet and diving suit for this purpose.

233. How did a certain New Mexico governor get his start in Florida?

Lew Wallace worked hard to invalidate the Baker County election returns with charges that Republican voters had been intimidated. The returns were invalidated and Hayes was given the electoral votes. The Republicans won Florida and Hayes became president. Wallace, later to become the author of *Ben Hur*, was made governor of New Mexico.

234. Who was William "Money" Williams?

"Money" Williams came from North Carolina to settle in Tallahassee in 1830 with a wagonload of money for starting a bank.

235. Who was the first territorial governor of Florida?

William P. Duval was the first territorial governor. He was appointed in 1822 and would serve a second time in 1834.

236. What major contribution did Governor Duval make to the City of Tallahassee?

He devised a town plan centered on Capital Square and had his Surveyor General, Benjamin Tennille, make a plan for the layout of the streets.

237. How did Call Street in downtown Tallahassee get its name?

It was named after Richard Call who was the Governor of Florida from 1836-39 and again from 1841–44.

238. How did Richard Keith Call earn his reputation?

Virginia-born Call fought as an officer in the army of Andrew Jackson in the War of 1812 and in the First Seminole War.

239. What famous words did Keith Call utter when he realized that Florida was bent on secession from the United States?

He said to the secessionists: "Well, Gentlemen, all I wish to say to you is that you have just opened the gates of hell!"

240. Which Governor of Florida was impeached four times but was never convicted?

It was Harrison M. Reed who was the ninth Governor of Florida. He served from July 4th, 1868 to January 7th, 1873.

241. What role did Francis Eppes play in the history of Tallahassee?

Francis Eppes was Thomas Jefferson's grandson. He took the position as reform mayor of Tallahassee in 1841, called at the time "intendent." He set about cleaning up the city. A fire may have helped him with the task.

242. With the history of Florida being divided between East and West Florida, who was mainly responsible for getting Florida accepted into the Union as a single state?

David Levy Yulee—a wealthy developer and politician—built a strong consensus and he was successful in getting Florida brought into the Union as a single entity. He became the first Jew in the country's history to hold the office of US Senator (1841–45)

243. What was the principal concern of the US Senate in voting for admission of territories as states in the 1840s?

The Senate wanted to keep the balance of votes between the free and slave states. Florida's entry as a slave state was balanced by Iowa's entry as a free state in 1846.

244. Who succeeded Governor Milton and how was this an unusual administration?

After Governor Milton's suicide, the President of the Senate, Abraham K. Allison became governor. This was a period of great unrest. Federal troops had to take charge and impose martial law. For a short time Governor Allison was imprisoned.

245. Who was Florida's Secretary of State from 1868–1873?

It was Jonathan Gibbs, an impressive black man from Philadelphia. He was considered the most cultured man in Florida government, having been educated at Dartmouth and Princeton.

The Civil War

246. What were the most important issues facing Florida politically during the antebellum years?

The main issues were slavery, industry-based tariffs and states' rights.

247. Why were the freedmen such a threat to the slave owners?

Many white slave owners looked upon freed Negroes as troublemakers and sources of rebellion. Discriminatory laws were passed to make life difficult for Florida's freedmen.

248. Under what conditions could Florida white slave owners free their slaves in 1845?

A law was passed making it illegal for Florida slaves to be freed unless they were given passage out of the state.

249. What was the two-state question concerning Florida as this territory sought statehood?

Many inhabitants wanted the territory to be admitted as two states—East and West Florida. This was similar to the British and Spanish models for their territories.

250. Why was the holding of slaves so important to Florida?

By 1850, population in the state had increased 30,000 from five years earlier. Close to half of the population was black. Slaves were essential to work the agriculture industries of cotton, turpentine and lumber.

251. What benefit in land did Florida receive when it entered the Union?

In 1851, when Florida entered the union, it received 500,000 acres of federal land. This land was transferred to state ownership.

252. What ship, originally named the Orento, became a ship of war for the Confederacy?

The British built the Orento for the Confederacy but refused to acknowledge it. The ship was renamed the Florida and was pressed into service for the South. Before being sunk in battle, it managed to capture about 70 ships for the South.

253. What Vice President of the United States became a fugitive from the law and had to leave the country?

John Breckinridge joined ranks with the South during the war and served as the Confederate Secretary of War. At war's end, he faced treason charges but fled abroad after a prolonged chase.

254. What was the resolution passed by the Democrats of Florida meeting in Jacksonville on May 15th, 1860?

The resolution stated that if the Union could not provide ample protection and security to slave property, that the banner of secession should be raised.

255. How supportive was the vote on Florida's secession from the Union?

On January 10th, 1861, a strong vote for secession was registered.

Sixty-two voted for secession and seven voted against it. Four of the seven votes against the movement came from West Florida where the non-slave position was the strongest. With this special ordinance passing in favor of secession, Florida became the third state to secede from the Union. Mississippi had seceded one day earlier.

256. When was the first offensive fought in the Civil War in Florida?

On the night of September 2nd 1861, a raiding party of confederates from Fort Pickens boarded the navy yard dry dock and burned the repair ship.

257. How did Governor John Milton face the financial problems at the beginning of the Civil War?

A county tax was levied for relief of dependents of servicemen; banks were permitted to suspend payments in specie for the war's duration; treasury notes and twenty-year bonds were put on sale with a high rate of interest.

258. How did Florida compare in size to other Confederate States?

Florida's population was still small. At the outbreak of the war, Florida's population was only 140,000. Florida was the least populous of the Confederate states. Relatively small numbers went to fight. Only about 15,000 men served in the Confederate Army. At the end of the war, about a third had been killed in combat or had died of disease.

259. What was the principal role Florida played during the Civil War?

Florida's principal role was that of producer of food for the southern armies.

260. Aside from food supplies for the Confederate Army, what other commodities did Florida provide?

Salt was of great importance during the Civil War to preserve meat supplies. Many Floridians were exempted from the draft to produce salt. In addition to salt, Florida supplied the Confederate Army with cattle and hogs.

261. What role did Fort Taylor play during the Civil War?

Fort Taylor's construction began around 1845 and the fort played an important role in holding Key West for the Union during the Civil War.

262. What war strategy did the Union Army adopt toward Florida from the beginning of hostilities?

In 1862, the federal forces began taking control of the Florida coast—Fernandina, St Augustine, Tampa, Jacksonville and Apalachicola in order to cut off food supplies and munitions.

263. What was General Lee's strategy for Florida during the war?

General Lee felt that it was critical to hold the interior of the state and protect the cattle ranches and farmlands.

264. What was the only major battle in Florida during the Civil War?

The only major battle was fought at Olustee near Lake City on February 20th 1864. A Confederate Army unit stopped the Union forces of about five thousand troops and drove them back to the coast.

265. What is the importance of the Natural Bridge State Historic Site?

At this location on March 5th, 1865, Confederate soldiers withstood a Union Army attack on St. Marks. There were heavy loses for the North. This battle saved the state capital of Tallahassee from being taken by the Union.

266. What was the date of the surrender of Florida's Confederate forces?

General Edward McCook entered Tallahassee on May 10, 1865 to accept the surrender of Florida's forces under Major General Jones.

267. How long did it take for news of Robert E. Lee's surrender at Appomattox, Virginia to reach Florida?

Word of the surrender did not reach Jacksonville for a whole week.

268. To quell the unrest in Florida after Appomattox, the federal government brought in troops. What angered the Floridians about this troop action?

The Union troops that marched into Florida were mostly black, which emphasized the completeness of the social revolution.

269. How did Governor Milton of Florida react knowing that the Confederacy would fall?

He declared that death would be preferable to enduring a return to the Union and its "loathsome embrace." On April 1st, 1865, Governor Milton killed himself with a fatal gunshot injury.

270. Who was the Florida citizen to conspire with John Wilkes Booth to assassinate Abraham Lincoln?

Lewis Powell met Booth in Baltimore. It was decided that while Booth was to shoot Lincoln, Powell was to attack Secretary of State William Seward. Powell stabbed Seward but the Secretary recovered from his wounds. Powell was executed, for his deed, in Washington on July 7th, 1865.

271. What single fact distinguished Tallahassee from the other capitals in the Confederacy?

Tallahassee was the only Confederate capital east of the Mississippi that had not been captured by Union forces by war's end.

272. How did Florida recover from the aftermath of the Civil War as compared to other Confederate states?

Carpetbaggers who plagued the South did not want to submit themselves to the torrid summers and diseases of Florida like malaria, typhoid, and dengue fevers. The winter months brought relief in financial terms to the state.

273. What were some of the negative results for the newly freed slaves in Florida after the war?

The freed slaves found themselves adrift, without education, specific training or employment. They had little means for finding work. Some returned to their former plantations and begged to be taken in.

274. What was the first useful assistance given to the freed slaves?

The Freedmen's Bureau, which was established by Congress in March 1865, gave assistance in the form of rations, help in organizing black schools and gave out information on their new rights.

275. What marked the first postwar state government in Florida?

With the inauguration of Governor David S. Walker in January 1866 came a series of repressive and harsh legislation, which were discriminatory towards Negroes.

276. How did the freed slaves of Florida react to their new freedom?

It was a difficult and confusing time for them during the transition. Nine-tenths of Florida's freed slaves returned to their former homes and worked in the fields but were paid for their labor. There was fear that, as soon as the federal forces left, the former slaves would be forced again into slavery.

277. What was the Black Code?

These were laws designed to regulate the lives of former slaves. In Florida one law provided the death penalty for any black who incited an insurrection. Death was also the penalty for the rape of a white woman and for stealing.

278. How were the labor shortage problems in the plantations met by former Supreme Court Chief Justice C. H. Du Pont?

In 1871, Judge Du Pont's plan was to import Swedish laborers who agreed to work for a year in the plantations. These men agreed to a salary of $120 for the year and proved to be excellent workers.

279. What role did Fort Jefferson play after the Civil War?

Fort Jefferson is the largest brick fort in the nation. It was never completed but it served as a prison after the Civil War. Its most famous prisoner was Dr. Samuel Mudd who was wrongfully accused of conspiracy and helping John Wilkes Booth with medical aid after he assassinated President Lincoln.

280. During Reconstruction what were the conditions that the US Government insisted on before readmitting southern states that seceded from the Union?

These states had to guarantee voting rights to Negroes. Florida's provisional government had earlier prohibited black voting rights and set up a series of Black Codes that further restricted and controlled the newly freed slaves.

281. What legislation served to separate the races in 1887 and virtually prevented the blacks from voting?

Jim Crow legislation separated the races and the poll tax excluded most blacks from being able to vote.

282. What single fact convinced white Floridians that the blacks should not be allowed to vote?

Many believed that blacks could not be educated, that they were inferior. These whites would take great pleasure in asking the blacks in front of a group of whites who the president of the country was or who the governor was. Most of the time the blacks could not answer.

283. The poll tax was one of the many ruses that white Floridians used to discourage blacks from voting. Why did many teachers who were in favor of black equality support the poll tax?

The teachers were put into a quandary because part of the money collected from the poll tax was earmarked for education.

284. How did Florida fare during the years of Reconstruction?

Financially, Florida fared better than most of the southern states. Florida gained the reputation of being a resort for invalids and tourists during the post-bellum years. When William Kelly, a Pennsylvania Congressman asked the question of how Floridians lived, he got a peculiar answer: "on sweet potatoes and consumptive Yankees."

285. What occurred to Florida's production of cotton in the years following the Civil War?

Production of cotton decreased about 30% compared to the pre-war years. Cotton acreage declined and farm values dropped.

286. When did Florida adopt a new constitution after the Civil War?

In 1868, Florida devised a new state constitution, which allowed its black citizens to vote. This was difficult for many Floridians to accept but this was a requirement of the US Government.

287. Where did Henry Flagler make his fortune prior to going to Florida?

Flagler made a fortune as a partner of John D. Rockefeller in Standard Oil. It was only after visiting St. Augustine in the winter of 1883 that he decided to remain in Florida to seek other opportunities. One of his greatest achievements was the East Coast Railway.

Religion

288. What ecclesiastical control did the churches in Florida come under in the 1500s?

In 1522, the Episcopal See of Santiago de Cuba was established. The Floridian Peninsula came under this authority.

289. How effective were the Spanish missions in Florida in converting the natives to Catholicism?

Between 1567 and 1705, eleven distinct Indian groups were affected by about 80 mission centers. By 1630, twenty thousand Indians had been baptized. This was the work of the Spanish Franciscans.

290. What was the first Protestant colony in the New World?

French Protestants seeking refuge from persecution settled in a location at the mouth of the St. Johns River. The year was 1562. The fort the French built for themselves was Fort Caroline. It was completed in 1564.

291. What was the fate of Fort Caroline?

In 1565, the Spanish destroyed Fort Caroline. Those French settlers, escaping the destruction of their homes were later massacred south of St. Augustine. Pedro Menendez de Aviles who had been ordered to kill all the Huguenots led the Spanish.

292. Who led the Huguenots?

The successor to Ribaut was a nobleman named René Laudonniere. He escaped the massacre, although wounded, and returned to France to write a history of the religious colony. In describing Ribaut's men during the first colony, Laudonniere wrote: "… the desolate continent … such privations as reduced the men to cannibalism."

293. At what point in Florida History did other religious denominations—besides Catholicism—begin to flourish?

Religious freedom began when the British occupied Florida. The Methodists settled in Pensacola in 1821 and the Baptists in Nassau County that same year. A few years later, the Presbyterians established themselves in St. Augustine. The Episcopalians came to St. Augustine in 1825.

294. Who was Dr. Cyrus Reed Teed?

Dr. Teed, a New York surgeon, started, through religious conviction, a colony for his faithful followers—about 200 in a community about 15 miles south of Fort Myers, called the Koreshan Unity. The followers denied themselves tobacco and liquor, believed in the wickedness of profanity and embraced celibacy. When the last of the original followers died, the land and all its buildings were deeded to the State of Florida.

295. Where was the first synagogue established in Florida?

Before building a large Jewish community in Miami, the Jews had already established themselves in Pensacola. Few Jews lived in Florida until after the Civil War. The first synagogue built in Pensacola was Temple Beth-El in 1874.

296. What historical importance is attached to the First Presbyterian Church in Tallahassee?

It's the city's oldest church, built in 1838. It's also important for African-Americans, as it was open for worship to slaves without prior consent of their owners.

Events and People of the 1900s and Later

297. What spouse of a Florida governor, in the first year of the new century, was instrumental in encouraging women to take a more active role in public life?

May Man Jennings, wife of William Sherman Jennings, became President of the Florida Federation of Women's Clubs. She worked for women's suffrage and conservation of natural resources.

298. What was the automobile speed record in the year 1903?

Alexander Winton established a new speed record at Daytona Beach with his gasoline-powered "Bullet." He traveled sixty-eight miles an hour.

299. What were the concerns of the first auto laws in Florida?

Auto drivers had to cede right of way to any person riding or leading a horse. On approaching bridges or curves, the autos had to reduce speed to four miles per hour. There were about 300 persons registered in Florida for automobiles in 1906.

300. How is Mary McLeod Bethune important to the education of blacks?

In October 1904, she opened her first school with six pupils, each paying fifty cents a week. She built her school to a worth of a million dollars. All this started with a desire to help improve the conditions of black laborers on Henry Flagler's East Coast railway.

301. On what kind of political platform did Napoleon Broward run?

In 1904, when Broward decided to run for governor, he decided his platform would be that of a friend of the people. He wanted to champion farmers, cattlemen, small businesses and labor against the overpowering urban corporate interests.

302. What background did Napoleon Bonaparte Broward bring to his bid for the post of governor?

He had been a logger and a farmhand as well as a cod fisherman in Newfoundland. He had also developed a phosphate mine.

303. What was the principal motivation for the passage of the comprehensive drainage law of 1905?

Governor Broward proclaimed that the drained area of the swampland would produce all the sugar needs of the entire country.

304. What was the purpose of the Buckman Act?

In 1905, a law was passed by the Florida legislature, which established an all-male University of Florida in Gainesville. The act also named the Florida State Normal and Industrial School as a land grant school for blacks.

305. What was the tuition at the University of Florida when it opened its doors in 1906?

Tuition was free for residents. Out-of-state students paid $20 a year. Dorm fees, at that time, were $2.50 a month. One hundred and two students enrolled the first year.

306. What is the origin of Tallahassee's newspaper?

In 1905, the city's two newspapers—*Capital* and *Tallahasseean* were consolidated into one newspaper, *The True Democrat*. John Collins shortened the name to *Democrat*.

307. Which Florida governor did so poorly in his studies that he flunked out of West Point?

When Broward ran for the United States Senate seat, Albert Gilchrist, a South Carolinian, ran for governor in 1908 and won. He had served in the Spanish-American War and had also served in the Florida House. As governor, he became a goodwill ambassador for Florida and traveled the country speaking of the wonderful opportunities and climate of the state.

308. What attempts did the Japanese make to establish a colony in Florida?

With the expansion of the railroad, a venture to establish a Japanese colony near present-day Boca Raton called Yamato was initiated. The goal was pineapple farming. A serious blight in 1908 destroyed the colony's prospects.

309. How did US newspapers stir up anti-Spanish sentiment before the Spanish-American War?

Joseph Pulitzer and William Randolph Hearst, through their newspapers told of Spain's ruthless suppression of the rebellion in Cuba and the atrocities against the Cuban people. Political clubs all over Florida collected money for the people of Cuba.

310. What was the point of embarkation for US troops for the invasion of Cuba?

Tampa Bay was the point where Teddy Roosevelt and his Rough Riders plus 23,000 troops left Florida for Cuba in 1898.

311. What journalist, in 1909, was responsible for sponsoring anti-Catholic sentiment in the state?

Tom Watson ran a series of articles in his *Jeffersonian Magazine* on the dangers of Roman Catholics in public office. He said that Catholics always put the church above the interests of the state.

312. What is the origin of the Miami Vizcaya Museum?

More than one thousand workers labored for two years to build this estate for millionaire James Deering, founder of International Harvester. The estate is now a museum that houses a collection of European art spanning 400 years.

313. What was the legacy of Governor Sidney J. Catts?

His election in 1916 halted Florida's advances in civil rights. He attacked Catholics and Negroes and made angry speeches, inciting religious intolerance.

314. During the First World War, what did President Wilson do in order to protect the long coastline of Florida?

In 1918, the President established three Defensive Sea Areas in Florida with bases in Key West, Tampa and Pensacola.

315. How many Floridians were in the armed services by the end of the First World War?

More than forty-two thousand Floridians were in the armed services at the time of the armistice. When the US declared war on Germany in 1917, Florida became immediately involved in naval and flying school initiatives. Submarine training was increased in Key West.

316. What was Florida's attitude toward Prohibition?

While Florida became an immediate supporter of the Volstead Act of 1919, the state was guilty of many of the infractions to the law. Florida, with its long coastline and its many coves, and its proximity to Cuba, became a major conduit for illegal liquor trade.

317. Who was the democratic governor who went to Florida to buy the newspaper *The Miami Metropolis*?

Ohio Governor James Cox ran for the US Presidency in 1920 with running mate Franklin Roosevelt. Cox lost the election to Harding. He then went to Florida and bought Miami's first newspaper and renamed it *The Miami Daily News*.

318. How is the name George E. Merrick connected with development?

What Henry Flagler did for railroads, Merrick did for real estate. He sold his first lot of land in what was later called Coral Gables in November 1921. In little time, he had more than 3000 salesmen working for him.

319. How did the Nineteenth Amendment to the US Constitution affect Florida?

Although the Amendment gave women the right to vote in 1920, Florida did not ratify the Amendment until 1969. However, Florida women began voting in 1920 and started, as well, to play a more important role in state affairs.

320. What peculiar method did farmers use to rid their cattle of tick fever in the 1920s?

State officials told farmers to dip their cattle into a solution of arsenic every two weeks. This procedure was discontinued because the arsenic got into the soil and then into the drinking water supply.

321. How did Alfred I. Du Pont profit from conditions in Florida in 1926?

He moved his legal residence to Florida that year and began purchasing land. He acquired about 70,000 acres in Franklin, Bay and Walton Counties. Du Pont also gained control of the Florida National Bank in Jacksonville.

322. To what was author Zora Neale Hurston referring when she wrote: "... It woke up old Okeechobee and the monster began to roll in his bed?"

Hurston was writing about the great storm of 1928 when the water of Lake Okeechobee flooded over its banks killing more than 2500 people.

323. What was the state of black religion during the years preceding the Great Depression?

There were approximately 3,000 black churches in Florida in 1926. The majority of African-Americans were members of the Baptist and African Methodists Episcopal churches.

324. When did the newspaperman William Randolph Hearst transport a Spanish monastery to the US?

The Spanish monastery, which was built in Seville, Spain between 1133 and 1141, was transported to the States in 1928.

325. How did Florida's anti-Catholic attitude influence the presidential elections of 1928?

Florida gave little support to Al Smith, a democrat and a Catholic. Herbert Hoover won the election with about 43,000 votes and carried Florida with about 57% of the popular vote.

326. Who was the Great Commoner?

William Jennings Bryan—a dynamic speaker in the 1920s, made his home in Florida. He was a devout fundamentalist who had a great influence on religious thought of his time.

327. How was the State of Florida important to Billy Graham?

As a young man, Billy Graham was delicate of health. His family moved to Florida for this reason. Billy enrolled in Bible studies.

He began to grow into his vocation and realized considerable success in the Tampa area and East Palatka.

328. How is the religious affiliation distributed throughout Florida today?

Unlike western states that were settled by Roman Catholic Missionaries who made great progress keeping that religion alive today, Florida, although having many Catholics, is primarily a Protestant state with considerable fundamentalist tendencies. The many different Protestant denominations combined make up the largest number. The Baptists and the Methodists are the most numerous. The Roman Catholics are the largest single block. The Jewish communities continue to grow, mostly in the Miami area.

329. What was the Rosewood Incident?

In Levy County, in the black township of Rosewood, a white woman claimed that a black man had raped her. She claimed that this man entered her home and assaulted her. A mob of more than 200 white men burned Rosewood to the ground. Many black residents were shot and others escaped into the swamps. It was January 1923.

330. What disasters hit Florida in the mid 1920s?

In 1926, the state suffered a great economic depression with many Floridians losing all their money and banks closing. Also in September of that year, a tremendous hurricane crumbled the dike of Lake Okeechobee. Hundreds died, many homes were destroyed and thousands were injured.

331. Where did circus master John Ringling build a mansion?

In order to find a place of rest for his traveling troupe of clowns and performers, John Ringling selected a site in Sarasota. He built a mansion designed after the Palace of the Doges in Venice, Italy. Today it has become a museum with a world-renown collection of European paintings.

332. Aside from the stock market crash of 1929, what other disaster hit Florida that year?

The European fruit fly devastated the citrus groves and destroyed 60% of the crop.

333. During Governor Carlton's administration, what significant art collection was willed to Florida?

The John and Mable Ringling Art Museum was opened in 1930, housing the finest art collection south of Washington, D.C.

334. Why did Alabama-born Claude Pepper lose his seat in the Florida legislature?

Attorney Pepper who represented Taylor County lost his seat in 1931 partly because he voted against a resolution to condemn Mrs. Herbert Hoover for inviting a black person to tea.

335. Did Claude Pepper's political career end in 1931?

No. Claude Pepper became a household name. He proved to be very effective in the Democratic Party and was elected to the US Senate for Florida.

336. What religious bigotry did John W. Martin show towards his opponent in the gubernatorial elections of 1932?

Martin was trying to prove his opponent David Sholtz was Jewish and had even written to Germany to get proof of that fact. In the second primary ballot, Sholtz beat Martin and also won the general election.

337. Who is Guiseppe Zangara?

On the evening of February 15th, 1933, Guiseppe Zangara made an attempt on the life of President-elect Franklin D. Roosevelt who was visiting Miami. Fortunately his aim was thrown off and Roosevelt was not hurt. Stray bullets, however, injured several bystanders.

338. In 1933, what was the first New Deal agency to begin operations in Florida?

The New Deal agency called the Civilian Conservation Corps (CCC) was the first. It made its initial project the reforestation of the Olustee National Forest. At first, CCC employed about 300 men for this job. Before long the one camp had grown to twenty-six throughout the state.

339. What do Al Capone and Esther Williams have in common?

They both stayed at the Biltmore Hotel in Coral Gables. Today it is a favorite of celebrities. The hotel has a Moorish tower and is lavishly furnished.

340. What was the most advantageous feature of the Wheeler-Howard bill passed in 1934?

The bill contained a provision to exempt the Seminoles from paying state and local taxes.

341. How did Florida begin to discourage transients from coming to the state in the 1934 post-depression era?

Governor Sholtz wired governors of the other southeastern states saying that Florida had no jobs to offer to transients and asked that they be discouraged from coming to relocate in Florida.

342. Where did author Marjorie Kinnan Rawlings make her home in Florida?

Rawlings, who won a Pulitzer Prize in 1939 for her book *The Yearling*, made her home in Cross Creek, about 20 miles southeast of Gainesville.

343. How did Carl Fisher respond to an invitation in July 1939 to a luncheon given by the Miami Beach Chamber of Commerce?

Carl Fisher, one of the main developers of Miami, was already in failing health in 1939 and he said, "You fellows at these luncheon parties live too high for me. I am on a diet of mainly pretzels and birdseed and some of these I have to take with a high pressure gun." Fisher, however, did attend the luncheon but he died on July 15th of gastric hemorrhage.

344. Who hosted the Duke and Duchess of Windsor on their occasional visits to Tallahassee?

The Duke and Duchess of Windsor were guests of their friend Mrs. George F. Baker at her Horseshoe Plantation in North Leon County.

345. Why is John D. Pennekamp remembered in the Florida Keys?

He was editor of *The Miami Herald* who championed the creation of the Everglades National Park. The nation's first underwater park near Key Largo is named after him.

346. How is Melvin Fisher remembered in the annals of Florida History?

Melvin Fisher is famous for his treasure hunting. He was very successful in salvaging Spanish galleons. His efforts brought gold up from the galleons Atocha and Santa Margarita, which sank off the Florida Keys in 1622.

347. When did the Mouse invade Central Florida?

Mickey Mouse and the Walt Disney World invaded Orlando in 1971. The Park is comprised of 27,400 acres in a community called Lake Buena Vista.

348. What was Janet Reno's position in state government from 1971 through 1973?

Janet Reno served as Staff Director of the Judiciary Committee of the Florida House of Representatives.

349. Where did Isaac Bashevis Singer make his home in Florida?

The Nobel Prize winner for literature in 1978 lived in Miami and taught at Miami University. He was known for his writings about his native Poland.

350. Who was the first Catholic Florida Governor?

In 1986, Bob Martinez of Tampa and former mayor of that city, was elected as the first Catholic governor of the state.

351. Where did Ray Charles study music after he lost his sight as a boy?

Ray Charles studied music at the St. Augustine School for Deaf and Blind Children.

352. What world-class tennis player is a native of Florida?

Chris Evert, native of Fort Lauderdale, is the first woman tennis player to earn one million dollars. She has won three Wimbledon and six US Open titles.

The Second World War and Beyond

353. How did Florida respond to the wartime need for facilities during the Second World War?

By April 1942, the Army Air Corps was making use of more than sixty thousand hotel rooms on Miami Beach. The army had established a training center, officer candidate school and officer training school.

354. What conditions made Florida an ideal location for military training during the war?

It was ideal for the jungle-like terrain and excellent weather. Florida had 172 military installations of various sizes.

355. How many Floridians were in uniform during the Second World War?

More than a quarter of a million Floridians took part as uniformed services personnel during the war.

356. What role did Fort Pierce play during this war?

Fort Pierce provided Naval Amphibious Training. More than 150,000 personnel were trained there.

357. To what extent did black soldiers participate during the war?

Although still segregated, the forces inducted over fifty thousand blacks into its ranks, which was about one-fifth of those serving for the state.

358. How did Florida meet its needs for agricultural laborers during the war?

Throughout the state, vagrancy laws were enforced and loafers were pressed into working for the citrus industry. The USDA signed agreements with the governments of the Bahamas and Jamaica to bring temporary immigrants to work in Florida agriculture.

359. What other ways did the Second World War bring prosperity back to the state?

In addition to the increased need for producing food, the establishment of military bases throughout the state helped improve the economy.

360. How did the Second World War help revitalize the City of Tampa?

The city had suffered greatly from the Great Depression and its cigar industry was gone. The construction of Mac Dill Air Field in 1939 and the shipbuilding industry helped revitalize the city.

361. What was the US and Allied Forces ship damage off the Florida coast during the war?

Twenty-four US and Allied freighters and tankers were sunk during the war. The German U Boats were responsible for this damage.

362. What German submarine action shocked the nation, just months after the attack by the Japanese on Pearl Harbor?

On February 19, 1942, a German submarine—U-128—entered the

Florida Straits and torpedoed and sank the US tanker Pan Massachusetts.

363. How did German spies land on the shore of Florida with explosives in 1942?

On June 18th, 1942, four German spies came ashore on Ponte Vedra Beach. They were found out and arrested. They were put to death on August 8th, 1942.

364. How many German prisoners of war were held in Florida during the war?

About three thousand POWs were kept in about fifteen labor camps throughout the state. Many were made to help harvest crops— fruit and vegetables.

365. Is there an instance when prisoners of war called a work strike?

A POW site at Camp Blanding near Starke sent its prisoners around the state on work details. To protest this, prisoners of Rommel's Afrika Korps staged a work strike in 1943.

366. How many Floridians were killed in combat during this war?

Of the 238,000 military personnel serving from Florida, almost five thousand were killed in combat.

367. What was Fred Cone's philosophy as governor of the state?

As the successor of Governor Sholtz, Fred Cone was not as liberal as the New Dealers would have liked. He believed in "lowering the budget to balance taxes instead of raising taxes to balance the budget." No increases were given to the schools.

368. What significant event brought increased revenue to Florida in September 1943?

Florida's first oil well came into existence that year in the Sunniland Field in northern Collier County. Prior exploration in the Pensacola area proved unfruitful.

369. What was the "Women's Emancipation Bill?"

This bill, passed in 1943, introduced by Representative May Lou Baker of St. Petersburg, assured the rights of married women to manage their separate estates, to sue and be sued independently of their husbands.

370. What was the farm policy called "No-fence?"

This was a long-standing policy to allow cattle to graze at will with hardly any restrictions. The farmers, wanting to protect their crops, fought against the cattle people to keep the livestock out of the cultivated fields. During the years 1949-50, legislation was passed to bar cattle from state and county roads and fenced properties. The era of the open-range cattle industry had come to an end.

371. How did republicans of Florida focus their attack on Senator Claude Pepper?

The popular democrat was brutally attacked with accusations of supporting the federal bureaucracy and organized labor, of coddling the blacks and of socialist tendencies. He was often called "Red" Pepper.

372. Did the democrats of Florida like General Dwight D. Eisenhower?

Everyone liked Ike. Claude Pepper even supported the move to induce Ike to run for president on the democratic ticket.

373. What was the focus of the Kefauver Crime Investigating Committee?

The 1950 Kefauver Crime Committee was trying to link open gambling to Governor Fuller Warren who had taken campaign funds from William H. Johnson, owner of Chicago and Florida racetracks.

374. When did the US Air Force launch its first missile from Florida?

The first missile was launched from Florida's Missile Test Center at Cape Canaveral in 1950.

375. What important civil rights activist was killed for his leadership of blacks in 1951?

In the late 1940s, Henry T. Moore led a movement to register blacks to vote. In December 1951, he was killed when his house was fire bombed by whites.

376. How are the years of Fuller Warren as governor evaluated in terms of statewide stability?

These were years of instability. There was illegal gambling as well as a wave of terrorist bombings of Negro homes and synagogues. The KKK was active. Although he allowed the passing of legislation that prohibited the wearing of masks by the KKK 1951, Warren left the governorship under a cloud in 1953.

377. What publication did Fuller Warren produce on politics?

Warren wrote a book entitled, *How to Win in Politics*. He believed that flowery speech would win support. He once said, "the goal of most orators is sound, not sense!"

378. Which Florida Governor suffered a heart attack less than two months after being sworn in?

Dan McCarty, Florida's 31st governor, was sworn in on January

6th, 1953 and suffered a heart attack on February 25th 1953. He continued to work, bedridden and died later that year from complications of a severe cold.

379. What experience did Leroy Collins bring to his run for governor in 1954?

Leroy Collins was a member of the Tallahassee legislature from 1934-54. He was determined to reinstitute the goals of the McCarty administration. Historians seem to agree that Collins' administration was one of the finest and most successful.

380. What ambitions did Leroy Collins have after six years as governor?

He wanted to run for the seat given up by Senator George A. Smathers. He did not succeed, partly because he had worked on President Lyndon Johnson's civil rights staff.

381. When did the civil rights movement get its start in Tallahassee?

Although the struggle of the blacks for equality was constant, the blacks began to boycott the city buses in May 1956.

382. Who was responsible for leading the bus boycott in Tallahassee?

It is generally accepted that Reverend C.K. Steele was the leader. Reverend Steele came from West Virginia and was very active in all aspects of the movement. He also helped in the establishment of the Southern Christian Leadership Conference.

383. Although Florida state politics have been primarily democratic in recent years, with the exception of Jeb Bush having been elected twice as governor, the candidates for President of the US, supported in Florida, have been mostly republican. What are the two notable exceptions?

Lyndon Johnson carried Florida in 1964 and Jimmy Carter in 1976.

384. What started the interest in horseracing in Florida?

As long as horses have been around, they have enjoyed running and racing each other. "Needles" was Florida's first Kentucky Derby winner, which may have started the profound interest in the state. Florida breeds about 9% of the nation's racehorses—about five thousand thoroughbreds a year.

385. What was the "Southern Manifesto" and how did Florida support it?

The Southern Manifesto, articulated in March 1956, pledged to use all lawful means to reverse the US Supreme Court's desegregation decision. At the time, Florida's two senators and six of its congressmen fully supported this action.

386. For what achievement is James Weldon Johnson known?

This Jacksonville lawyer and statesman wrote the song, "Lift Every Voice and Sing." This is known as the Black National Anthem.

387. What chain eating facility did the blacks target for their sit-in lunch demonstrations?

Woolworth's lunch counters were targeted to protest against segregated eating facilities in 1960.

388. When was the first rocket launching the first American into space?

In 1961, Alan Shepard was launched in a rocket from Cape Canaveral.

389. What event in 1962 had a chilling effect on tourism in Florida and caused great concern to the rest of the nation?

Of great danger to the United States was the Cuban/Russian Missile Crisis.

390. What was the goal of the "swim-ins" held in St. Augustine?

In 1964, black Americans were eager to desegregate Florida beaches. They targeted St. Augustine during the city's 300th year celebration. This action brought Congress to pass the Civil Rights Act.

391. Who was the first black to receive a degree at Florida State University?

Max Courtney was the first black to receive his degree in August 1965.

392. What important issues do black Floridians face today?

Their struggle for civil rights has been long and difficult. Today, blacks are still concerned about housing segregation and equal income with whites. Unemployment among blacks is still almost three times that of whites in Florida.

393. Who was the first republican governor for Florida since Reconstruction?

Claude Kirk broke the string of democratic governors with the support of US Senator Ed Gurney and President Nixon.

394. When did Apollo 11 take off from the Cape?

Apollo 11 lifted off from the Cape on July 16th, 1969.

395. How are the decades of the 1950s and 1960s remembered most in Florida?

The 1950s were marked by tremendous population growth. In those years, the population of Florida increased by 78.8 percent. The 1960s were marked by the growth of NASA for the space industry on Merritt Island. In 1969, NASA put the moon within our reach.

Education

396. What was the first school developed in what today is the United States?

In 1573, Franciscan missionaries settled in St. Augustine. In 1605, they established a seminary—the first school in the United States.

397. When did Florida's first free public school open?

The state's first free public school opened in St. Augustine in 1831 but soon afterwards closed because of a lack of funds.

398. When was state-supported higher education approved in Florida?

A state-supported higher education law for white students was passed in 1851. The law provided for seminaries in East and West Florida. The East Florida institution began at Gainesville in 1853. The West Florida institution was started in Tallahassee in 1856.

399. From what origins does Florida State University (FSU) descend?

FSU's early origin was the West Florida Seminary, which opened in 1857.

400. At what point in history did Florida's peninsula to the south begin to develop?

It was not until the 1880s that Florida began to expand towards the south—mostly because of the establishment of the railroads.

401. Why is Miami constantly referred to as a young city?

Miami was little more than a fishing village in 1896 and did not begin its development until the 1920s. In truth, the city is less than one hundred years old.

402. What are perhaps the three greatest drawbacks to living in the Miami area today?

First, because of its location, between the Everglades and the Atlantic Ocean, the area is subject to frequent flooding. Secondly, despite the serious controls, the onslaught of mosquitoes is always troublesome. Thirdly, crime is still high and causes residents and visitors concern.

403. When did state-supported funds become available for African-Americans?

Under Governor Bloxham, an annual appropriation was approved for black students in 1883.

404. When was Rollins College established?

In 1884, Winter Park won the bid to establish Rollins College. In support of this institution, the town offered $125,000 in land and cash. The college was named after its largest benefactor, Alonzo Rollins and opened in 1885.

405. What were the name changes of Florida State University over the years?

In 1890, the institution was known as West Florida Seminary. In 1901, it became Florida State College. The name changed to the

Florida State College for Women in 1905. In 1947, it became Florida State University.

406. What was the "separate but equal" doctrine?

The US Supreme Court enunciated this doctrine in 1896. This doctrine was flawed in that the schools remained separated but were definitely not equal. School facilities for blacks were sorely substandard; the length of academic years was shorter for blacks than for whites. These conditions reflected the Jim Crow frame of mind in Florida and throughout much of the South.

407. How did religious denominations support private education in Florida during the late 1800s and early 1900s?

The Florida Baptist Convention began Stetson University in 1883. The Methodists funded Florida Southern College in a new site near Clearwater in 1906.

408. How much did Florida Southern College pay Frank Lloyd Wright for his master plan for designing the buildings on the campus?

The College President of Florida Southern, Ludd M. Spivey, paid the architect $13,000 for the master plan. Later the College paid Wright, as it collected donations for the project, another $100,000.

409. Just after the turn of the century, what was the prevailing disparity between white and black teaching salaries?

Black teachers, for example, in Gainesville were making about $500 a year while white teachers were earning about $900.

410. How did Florida compare with the other states in matters of education in the early 1930s?

Florida was sorely deficient in many areas. It ranked forty-third in the nation for teachers' salaries and thirty-ninth in the amount of money spent for students annually. By the end of the decade, in the late 1930s, federal funds were made available for rebuilding and refurbishing the public schools in Florida. Works Progress Administration (WPA) did a good bit of the enhancement.

411. How were the institutions of higher education affected in the post World War II Era?

There was a great shortage of facilities. The University of Florida, for example, received more than 8,000 applications for admission in the summer of 1946. There were many more students than the university had planned for. These applications came mostly from ex-service members, taking advantage of government assistance.

412. What were the results of the 400-page report on the state of education in Florida in 1947?

This report "Education and the Future of Florida" rated Florida third from the bottom of all the other states. Funding for schools was found to be seriously inadequate.

413. Who was Zora Neale Hurston?

She was one of the first writers to celebrate the black experience in rural agricultural Florida.

414. Who was John Gilbert?

John Gilbert was a black teacher who decided to file a lawsuit in Brevard County for the unequal pay given to black teachers. The year was 1937. Four years later, a federal judge ruled for equal pay for black teachers.

415. How long did it take for Florida's schools to integrate after the US Supreme Court ordered desegregation?

After the ruling of the Supreme Court in 1954, it took eighteen years before all Florida schools were integrated.

416. What were the four institutions of higher education open to blacks prior to 1958?

The only institutions available to blacks prior to 1958 were: Florida Agricultural and Mechanical University (FAMU), Bethune-Cookman College, Florida Memorial and Edward Waters College.

417. When were the University of Florida graduate schools finally opened to black students?

On June 18th 1958, Federal District Court Judge Dozier de Vane ordered the graduate schools opened to blacks.

418. How many accredited institutions are there in Florida?

There are more than 35 regionally accredited colleges and universities in both the private and public domains.

419. How many institutions make up the state university system in Florida?

There are, at present, ten institutions that make up the state university system. The University of Florida is the largest.

420. When was the largest Cuban immigration to Florida?

In 1980, approximately 125,000 Cuban refugees came to Florida during the Mariel boatlift.

421. How did this influx of people aggravate black and white race relations?

Along with the racial rioting that year in Florida, blacks were afraid and angry that the influx of so many Cubans would take jobs away from African-Americans.

422. What was the approximate number of Cubans to immigrate to Florida during the 1950s, 1960s and again in the 1980s?

During these decades, more than 430,000 Cubans came to Florida.

423. Why was it so difficult to form unions for workers in Florida's agriculture?

On one hand, there was strong resistance from farm owners. On the other hand, it was difficult to keep in touch with these workers because they only worked seasonally, were mostly uneducated and had no permanent addresses.

424. What brought the Haitians to Florida?

In 1981, hundreds of Haitians fled the repressive Duvalier government and landed in Florida near Key West. Since then many Haitians have sought a home in Florida for reasons other than political ones.

425. What were some of the negative aspects to unprecedented population growth from diverse regions?

Natural resources were strained; crime and violence grew to troubling levels. In the early 1980s, a grand jury claimed that about 73% of illegal drugs entered the US through southern Florida.

426. What was the date of the first space shuttle disaster?

In 1986, the space shuttle Challenger exploded shortly after takeoff. All seven crewmembers were killed.

427. What great natural disaster destroyed south Florida and Homestead Air Force Base?

In 1992, Hurricane Andrew destroyed everything in its path with damages estimated at 30 billion dollars.

428. What are some of the reasons given for the high crime rate in Florida?

Some blame the low wages workers earn and a niggardly spending welfare system. Some feel that the reasons go back to Florida's indifference to school funding. Others feel that there was a breakdown in traditional family values. Often, where there is great diversity in population, there is high crime. Florida brings in many tourists each year, which may be viewed as easy picking for thieves.

429. When did Florida host the Summit of the Americas?

In December 1994, Miami hosted the largest gathering of world leaders this country had assembled to date.

Other Places of Importance

430. How long did St. Augustine serve as the capital of colonial East Florida?

Through the years under threat and frequently sacked by pirates, burned by the British and ravaged by yellow fever, St. Augustine served as capital of colonial East Florida for 259 years.

431. What is considered the oldest area in Florida in regards to foreign occupation?

Northeastern Florida, including Amelia Island existed under eight different flags over four centuries.

432. What is the peculiarity of the coast directly south of Tallahassee?

The coast is a natural wetland habitat. St. Marks National Wildlife refuge is here. The refuge is comprised of more than 65,000 acres and is home to about 300 bird species and more than fifty types of reptiles and amphibians.

433. When did Tallahassee become the permanent capital of Florida?

Three years after Florida became a territory of the US in 1821,

Tallahassee became the permanent capital of the state. Tallahassee is considered the most isolated capital in the nation. It lies 170 miles from Jacksonville; 200 miles from Pensacola; 240 miles from Tampa; 240 miles from Orlando and 460 miles from Miami.

434. What economic boom made Apalachicola the third largest port on the Gulf?

Cotton was responsible for this great boom. From Apalachicola, riverboats transported cotton to the north and abroad.

435. Why is Fort Pickens an important historical site today?

Although Fort Pickens played a relatively unimportant role during the Civil War, this Pensacola fort was used as a holding area for Geronimo, the captured Apache leader in 1866. It is rumored that Geronimo made money from tourists by cutting off the buttons from his coat and selling them. He would sew on more at night for the next day's sale.

436. Who were the first settlers of the City of Orlando?

The first white settlers were soldiers who decided to remain in that area after the Seminole wars in 1830. Orlando remained a quiet little town until business moved there after the railroads came south.

437. What is the oldest standing church in Florida?

It is Old Christ Church in Pensacola. It was built in 1832. During the Civil War, it was used by Union soldiers as a barracks and a hospital.

438. What is the origin of Panama City?

In 1838, James Watson acquired the land and developed what is today Panama City.

439. How did Panama City get its name?

One story tells of George Mortimer West, a promoter from Chicago, who vacationed in the area while the Panama Canal was being constructed. He told his friends that by drawing a line from Chicago to the Panama Canal, it would pass through the coast at the point that he then called "Panama City."

440. What was St. Augustine's importance aside from being the oldest city in the United States?

St. Augustine was the center of the citrus industry for some time after the Spanish introduced this crop to Florida. In 1835, however, after a long-lasting freeze killed all the trees, the industry moved south.

441. How did the Yulee Sugar Mill Historic Site get its name?

David Yulee, a former US senator and the first Jew from Florida to hold such a position, operated this mill for 13 years beginning in 1851. He supplied the Confederate Army with sugar products until 1864, when the mill and Yulee's house were burned to the ground.

442. What interest does Ybor City have for visitors to Florida?

Ybor City is an enclave of Tampa. Many Cubans call this city their home. In 1886, Cubans brought their cigar-making industry to Ybor.

443. How did this industry grow?

Martinez Ybor began making cigars in 1886. His small business grew into an enormous one with fifty factories. The city took his name—Ybor. At the height of their productivity, the factories employed about 200,000 people. Today, there are perhaps less than fifty people who can make cigars in the old tradition in Tampa.

444. What is Florida's "Big Scrub?"

This is the Ocala National Forest, which covers 430,000 acres and is the oldest national forest east of the Mississippi. It is the only forest in Florida with subtropical vegetation.

445. Where is the Naval Live Oaks Reservation?

It is located at Seashore Gulf Islands. In 1828, President John Quincy Adams set aside 1,400 acres of live oak timber for building naval vessels.

446. What is the historical significance of Castle Warden?

William G. Warden, one of the partners of John D. Rockefeller, built it in 1887. Warden built this structure instead of investing with Henry Flagler in the railroads, which Warden considered a poor investment. Today Castle Warden houses Ripley's Believe It or Not Museum and continues to be one of Gainesville's finest tourist attractions.

447. Why is the Gamble Plantation important historically?

Robert Gamble purchased this plantation in 1840. With more than 200 slaves, Gamble established a sugarcane plantation and refinery. Ten years later, when sugar prices plummeted, he sold out. During the Civil War, Confederate soldiers used the plantation as a supply station. After the war, Judah P. Benjamin used the plantation home as a hideout.

448. How did the Walton area of Florida get its name?

Walton County was named after Colonel George Walton, Secretary of West Florida. The Euchee and Choctaw Indian tribes once inhabited this area.

449. What great feat does the Overseas Highway conceal in its past?

Henry Flagler's greatest project was to build a railroad from Florida City to Key West. The terrible hurricane of 1935 destroyed the railroad but today the Overseas Highway follows or parallels Flagler's great accomplishment.

450. Where was the first railroad line in Florida?

The first railroad line extended between Tallahassee and St. Marks. It was completed in 1836 and stretched for twenty-three miles.

451. Why is the site of the State Museum of San Marcos de Apalachee of historical interest?

This was the location where Panfilo Narvaez arrived with 300 men in 1528. The spot marks the confluence of the Wakulla and St Marks Rivers.

452. What is the "Alcatraz of the Army?"

In Lanark Village, east of Carrabelle, there was once a World War Two training camp. This was called Camp Gordon. Walter Winchell called it "The Alcatraz of the Army" for its isolation and rigorous demands on the trainees. Today Lanark Village is a retirement community.

453. What role did Station "J" play during the Second World War?

Station "J" stands for Lighthouse Jupiter, which is located on the Intracoastal Waterway. Its main purpose during the war was to locate German submarines in the Atlantic Ocean. General George Meade who later made his mark during the Civil War at Gettysburg designed this lighthouse in 1860.

454. How did the City of Orlando get its name?

It is believed that the city got its name from Orlando Reeves. Reeves was a soldier who, while on sentinel duty, managed to warn the camp of an Indian attack but died to save his fellow soldiers.

455. For what is the town of Monticello, Florida best known?

The Monticello Opera House is known throughout the US as a marvelous 1900s Victorian structure. Although closed down for many years, it now has a full schedule of events during the year.

456. What was the original name for the city of Jacksonville?

Jacksonville began as Cowford. This was where herds of beef cattle crossed the St. Johns River. Today Jacksonville is one of the state's largest cities and one of the nation's busiest ports. In landmass, Jacksonville is the largest city in the United States with 840 square miles.

457. Why is Fort Gadsden considered an historical site?

Fort Gadsden lies just thirty miles from Apalachicola. The fort was held by the British during the War of 1812 to recruit Seminole Indians and Negroes to fight against the US forces. The US troops destroyed the fort, killing hundreds of people. The fort was later made into a supply depot.

458. Why was St. Marks' Lighthouse reconstructed twice in a period of twelve years?

The tower was built in 1829 with hollow walls, rather than solid ones. The tower was reconstructed in 1831. In 1842, a new tower was built because the soil under the original one had started to erode.

459. When did the city sidewalks of Tallahassee get paved?

During the decade of 1910–20, the city limits were expanded and voters approved bonds to pave the downtown sidewalks.

460. When did Tallahassee get its first taxi service?

The first taxi service was established in 1914 in the capital with a strict speed limit of ten miles per hour.

461. Where is Gold Dust Street in Tallahassee?

Gold Dust Street lies on three blocks of Calhoun Street between Tennessee and Georgia Streets. This is an historic district with elaborate old homes belonging to prominent citizens around the years 1830-1880.

462. What is the origin of the "Hemingway House" in Key West?

The house was a gift to Ernest and his second wife Pauline Pfeiffer from her uncle Gus in 1931. Hemingway remained in Key West for eleven years before moving on to wife number three.

463. How did the Tamiami Trail get its name?

The highway linking Miami to Fort Myers and then north to Tampa was named in 1915 "Tamiami" for Tampa—Miami. It was not until 1928 that the road became a reality.

464. In what way is Fort Lauderdale compared to Venice, Italy?

Like Venice, one can travel by water-taxi or taxi-boat to the many docks along the city's waterways.

465. What is the nation's largest marine park?

This is Biscayne National Park. It was established in 1968 as a national monument. Twelve years later, it expanded into a marine park as well. The entire park is comprised of 274 square miles. A small portion of it consists of mainland coast.

466. What is unusual about the Sunshine Skyway?

This is one of the nation's longest highways completely over water. This fifteen-mile stretch links the Bradenton area with St. Petersburg.

467. What brought prosperity to the Panhandle of Florida in the 20th century?

The area was virtually unknown prior to World War Two when military bases were built there. Beach property was very cheap prior to 1940, selling for about one hundred dollars an acre. Today, the same acre would fetch tens of thousands of dollars.

468. What industry was Cedar Keys known for in the post-Civil War years?

This area had three pencil factories, which processed 300 logs per day, creating pencil stock for shipment to the North and Europe.

469. In which Florida town is the Salvador Dali Museum located?

The Dali Museum is in St. Petersburg.

470. How did such a relatively small Florida town become the home of many of the works of Dali?

Ohio millionaire A. Reynolds Morse, a good friend of Dali, started the collection with many of his own collected works, and selected St. Petersburg because it had tourist potential.

471. How did the town of Havana, near Tallahassee, get its name?

It was named for the capital of Cuba. This town northwest of Tallahassee began the cultivation of Cuban tobacco in 1829.

472. Which cities in Florida suffered the most during the yellow fever epidemics of the late 1880s?

The cities hardest hit by the yellow fever epidemic were Key West, Manatee, Plant City and Jacksonville. Jacksonville lost about four thousand people to yellow fever.

473. How did the inhabitants attempt to purify the air during the yellow fever epidemic?

During the yellow fever epidemic of 1887, efforts were made to drive away the disease by setting fires of pine and tar. Lime and disinfectant were applied to tree trunks and posts. Streets were sprayed with bichloride of mercury.

474. What made Pensacola such an important Florida town on the Panhandle?

Pensacola, along with Apalachicola and St. Joseph were important Gulf port towns. A hurricane and yellow fever destroyed St. Joseph in 1841.

475. On what location did the University of Tampa settle?

It was originally the Tampa Bay Hotel built by Henry B. Plant. Plant, a native of Connecticut, was known for his railway lines from the Atlantic Port of Jacksonville to the Gulf at Tampa.

476. What was Florida's most exclusive winter resort in the late 1880s?

Henry M. Flagler built the Ponce de Leon Hotel in St. Augustine in a lavish Spanish-Moorish style, which became a mecca for the very wealthy.

477. What is an Afromobile?

Henry Flagler used Afromobiles in his hotels. They were two-wheel rickshaws powered by the physical energy of blacks.

478. What preceded the custom of using the beaches of Daytona for automobile trials?

Prior to the use of automobiles on the Daytona Beach, inhabitants would walk, bike ride or buggy ride on the beach.

479. How did one of Cuba's finest art collections find its way to Daytona Beach?

Cuba's Strongman Batista was a collector, among other things and donated many paintings to the National Gallery in Cuba. When he realized that Fidel Castro was going to take over the country, Batista sent many of the paintings to Daytona Beach where he had sent his wife and children. Batista, however, was unable to follow them because President Eisenhower refused to give the ex-dictator asylum in the US.

480. What happened to all the lime groves that the Keys were known for years ago?

Large commercial groves, which supplied significant quantities of limes to the nation, were destroyed by hurricanes in the 1920s and 1930s. In their place, hotels and private homes sprouted.

481. Where in Central Florida can one enjoy scenes of the Serengeti Plain and its exotic animals?

Busch Gardens allows visitors to see more than 3000 animals in a setting of Africa. There are giraffes, zebras, elephants and many other animals that roam free and can be viewed from the safety of a monorail.

482. Why was the city of Tallahassee selected as the Territorial Capital?

Tallahassee was the convenient halfway location between St. Augustine and Pensacola.

483. What were the complaints about keeping the capital in Tallahassee?

From before the Civil War, Tallahassee was considered too remote, not large enough or prosperous enough or lacking sufficient hotels and restaurants. In 1881, a bill was introduced to look for a more appropriate city to serve as the State Capital. Governor Bloxham vetoed the measure and was able to get the support of the legislature.

484. When was the present capitol built?

The original building of the present capitol was completed in 1845, just prior to having Florida attain statehood. The dome was built in 1849. Additions to the structure were made through 1947.

485. Where was the first capitol building located?

The first capitol building was located on old Apalachee land in Indian fields. It was a log cabin. The third legislative session met there in 1824.

486. What famous Tallahassee house became a museum and later was known as the "House That Rhymed?"

Lu Ella Knott gave her home to the city. It has become the Knott House Museum. Lu Ella Knott wrote poetry about all the furniture in her house; so, it became known as the House That Rhymed.

487. What city in Florida is considered the sunniest in the entire state?

The Guinness Book of Records recognizes St. Petersburg as having the longest string of consecutive sunny days—a total of 768.

488. Where in the state were troops trained for the Bay of Pigs Invasion?

Troops were trained on the Island of Useppa (known at one time as Joseffa) in southwest Florida. It's considered the oldest continuously occupied landmass on the Western Florida coast.

489. Which Florida city is called "the working son in the Florida family of playboys?"

Jacksonville is the most industrialized city in the state and is the largest city in landmass in the United States.

490. What peculiar characteristics does the Monument of States in Kissimmee have?

The monument is made of stones taken from every state in the US as well as many foreign countries. The monument was built in 1943.

491. What is unique about Hialeah Park?

Aside from being Florida's oldest horseracing palace, Hialeah Park is home to the spectacular flamingoes, living in a park comprised of 220 acres. In 1931, flamingos were brought there from Cuba and released. At first, they flew off. After initially attempting to clip their wings, the keepers now find that the flamingos have willingly made their home there.

492. Where was history made with the first scheduled commercial airplane flight in the world?

The first scheduled commercial flight took place in 1914 between St. Petersburg and Tampa. The pilot was Tony Jannus and his aircraft was a seaplane.

493. What part of the huge Okefenokee Swamp extends into Florida?

This swamp straddles the Georgia-Florida border. Only 66 square miles of its 660 square miles extend into Florida.

494. Where is Florida's smallest post office?

Florida's smallest post office is also the nation's smallest post office. It's in Ochopee in the Everglades. It's eight feet four inches long by seven feet three inches wide.

495. Where is the smallest police station in the world?

This police station is nothing more than a telephone booth with a squad car parked outside. It's in Carrabelle, Florida on the Panhandle Coast.

496. Where is Florida's famous Butterfly World?

Butterfly World is west of Fort Lauderdale, inside Tradewinds Park. This three-acre site is home to 80 butterfly species from South and Central America and Asia.

497. What are the designated Canopy Roads in Leon County?

These are the official Canopy Roads in the county: The Old Bainbridge Road, The Old St. Augustine Road, Miccosukee Road, Centerville Road, Moccasin Gap Road, Magnolia Road and Meridian Road.

498. Where is the Annual Seafood Festival held?

The Panhandle sponsors the Annual Seafood Festival. It's held at Battery Park in Apalachicola during the month of November.

499. How is Ft. Myers associated with baseball?

The Boston Red Sox play at Ft. Myers during its spring training.

500. What distinction does Florida have college football?

Florida hosts more college football bowl games than any other state in the country. The best-known are: the Orange Bowl in Miami and the Citrus Bowl in Orlando.

501. Where was the first Orange Bowl game played?

In 1933, it was called the Palm Festival, a forerunner to the Orange Bowl. The game was played at Moore Park, which held a 3000-seat grandstand.

502. Where did the sport Jai alai have its origins?

This sport, which is played all over the Latin world as well as in Florida and states of the Southwest, began in the Basque Country of Spain. In Spain the game is known as "Pelota." It's considered the world's fastest game with the ball traveling more than 170 miles an hour.

503. Where is the International Swimming Hall of Fame?

This Hall of Fame is in Fort Lauderdale. Pictures of the world's greatest swimmers including Johnny Weissmuller, Esther Williams and Mark Spitz are shown here with their honors.

504. Where in Florida did the filming of several Tarzan movies take place?

This jungle-like setting is in Wakulla Springs, south of Tallahassee. At Wakulla Springs, 600,000 gallons of water gush out every minute.

505. Where can scuba divers spend the night in an under-water lodge?

This unusual site is at Jules' Undersea Lodge near Key Largo. Divers can spend the night in a two-room hotel, 30 feet below the surface of the water.

506. Where is the Annual Festival of the Five Flags held?

This annual festival celebrated each June in Pensacola recognizes that Florida, during its history, lived under five different country flags—Spain, France, Great Britain, the Confederacy and the United States.

507. Is it true that Orlando was not Walt Disney's first choice for his Florida theme park?

It is believed that Disney first considered northwest Florida but was prevented from buying land there. Ed Ball of the St. Joe Paper Company, it is rumored, refused to sell the land.

508. Has anyone, during the course of Florida history, ever envisioned building a canal joining the Atlantic Ocean to the Gulf of Mexico by going through Florida?

The early Spaniards first considered it. Thomas Jefferson was the first president to express an interest. Several US Presidents since then considered such a canal but the project never materialized. Finally President Nixon put the matter to rest when it was predicted that such a waterway would endanger the water supply of the peninsula below such a canal.

509. How many jobs has Disney World provided to residents of Florida?

About forty thousand Floridians now work at Disney World and they help entertain more than thirty million tourists each year.

510. What attraction preceded Disney World in Central Florida?

The oldest continuous attraction in that region is Cypress Gardens build by Dick and Julie Pope.

511. What can visitors see at the Kennedy Space Center?

The Visitor's Center is located just south of Titusville on the Central Florida Coast. One can visit the Gallery of Space Flight, NASA Art Exhibit and the Outdoor Rocket Garden.

Florida Population, Growth and Size

512. What are the distances East and West and North and South of Florida?

The greatest distances in both directions are almost the same. They exceed 450 miles. Florida's land area is 58,560 square miles.

513. How far is Key West from Cuba?

Key West, the last island in the Keys, is only ninety miles from Cuba.

514. Does Florida have the longest coastline in the United States?

Florida has the second longest coastline after Alaska.

515. How does Florida compare in size with the other 49 states?

There are 21 states larger and 28 states smaller than Florida.

516. What year did Florida have its largest land boom?

In 1925, about 2.5 million people bought land to make Florida their permanent residence.

517. What was the impetus for the land boom?

With the arrival of the railroads, land was snatched up quickly for vacation resorts, especially along the coast. Prior to tourism, land was purchased for plantations and orange groves.

518. What is the high mark for immigration into Florida?

The decade of the 1980s had a daily immigration that averaged 900 people.

519. What events contributed to making Florida more accessible for travel?

In the 1880s, the railroads served this function. Today air travel makes Florida more accessible to the rest of the nation and beyond. There are more than five hundred designated airfields in the state. The busiest airports are: Miami, Tampa, Orlando and Jacksonville.

520. What is the current population of Florida?

The population in Florida exceeds 15 million. The state is fourth in size in the US after California, Texas and New York.

521. What is meant by the old adage "Florida is the only northern state in the deep South?"

If one were to draw a line across the center of the state, one would find that everything south of it is northern and everything north of it is southern.

522. How does the population of Florida increase each year through tourism?

Because of the magnificent beaches, sunny weather and recreation parks, Florida gets about 45 million tourists each year who spend more than 20 billion dollars.

523. In relative terms, how has Florida's population grown during the years 1950-1980?

In 1950, Florida ranked twentieth in size in the nation. In 1980, Florida was fourth in size.

524. How did Miami Beach's foreign population differ from that of the foreign population average for the rest of the state in 1960?

Miami Beach had a foreign-born population of about 33%, mostly East Europeans and Jewish immigrants, while the state average was about 5.5%.

525. How did the events of 1980 change the makeup of the population of South Florida?

The Mariel Boatlift brought many Cuban exiles to this area. In Dade County, the 1990 census reported about 45% foreign born.

526. What makes Miami so ethnically diverse?

The population includes African-Americans, Asians, Cubans Haitians and Jews from many foreign countries and the US. There are more than 24,000 Haitians in Florida who fled poverty and political repression, as did many Cubans.

527. What was the principal obstacle to Bahamian immigration, and for that matter, Haitian immigration?

Throughout the last decades of the 1800s through the first four decades of the 1900s, the principal obstacle for blacks was racial segregation and discrimination. There is an unfortunate history of police confrontation with these people.

528. What was the population of Florida at the time of statehood?

In 1845, the population of Florida was approximately 54,000 people, almost half of which were slaves.

529. What was the principal cause for the population boom in Tallahassee between 1825 and 1840?

The population in Tallahassee grew from 996 in 1825 to more than 11,000 in 1840. The rich land brought farmers, planters and slaves to the area.

530. What proved to be the great impetus for growth in Tampa?

In 1892, there were 1000 residents in Tampa. The American Tobacco Company started making cigars in 1891. In the decades that followed, population increased more than 150% while the average for the state was 35% to 42%.

531. How did the Spanish American War contribute to further population growth in Florida?

Returning soldiers from Cuba were attracted by the climate and beautiful coastlines and decided to remain in Florida.

532. Where is the greatest density of population in Florida?

Ninety-one percent of the population lives in metropolitan areas. The densest is in the southeast complex between Miami and West Palm Beach. The average density in the state is 240 people per square mile.

533. What percentage of the overall Florida population is African American?

About 14% of the population is African-American. Florida cities are less economically segregated than the typical US city; African

Americans fill about one in seven managerial or professional positions.

534. What did the Census of 2000 figures show in terms of older citizens, sixty years old and up?

In the year 2000, there were 3,582,823 senior citizens in the state.

535. How did the growth rate differ in Florida during the 1900s through the year 2000 compared with the growth rate average in the US?

Florida experienced a growth rate during this period of 20% compared to 10.5% rate in the rest of the US.

536. How can one summarize the overall growth rate in population over the years?

Florida reached a population of almost a million in 1910. Forty years later the population had tripled. In the following twenty years, the population tripled again. Between 1970 and 1990, the population rose from 6.8 million to 13 million.

537. How do Floridians feel about the continual increase in population?

About 70% of the population believes Florida's overcrowding and overpopulation is a major problem. About 60% believe that adding as little as another five million would be as serious matter.

538. Which Florida town is the most affluent per capita?

Palm Beach is the most affluent, not only in Florida but also in the entire nation.

Conclusion

The questions I have selected for inclusion in this book are representative of the thousands of such queries one can make on the subject. Perhaps more emphasis has been put on the history of Florida than other topics because I have found it to be fascinating. One cannot understand Florida's history in isolation. It is part of a greater whole, of historical developments involving other nations and their interests throughout most of the Eastern, Southern and Southwestern regions of the United States.

Like California, New Mexico and Texas, Florida was of great interest to Spain. And Florida, like these regions, failed to yield the wealth in precious stones and metals that Mexico and Peru had provided. The search for this wealth was the primary motivating force for exploration. None of the original settlers could anticipate that the regions which had profoundly disappointed them would, in time, prove to be of enormous value. Whereas New Mexico was sufficiently isolated from other outside incursions until well into the eighteen hundreds, Florida was coveted by the British and the French from the very beginning of the Spanish settlements in the fifteen hundreds.

In all these regions, the Catholic Church built missions and put the natives to work in order to save their souls. The Spaniards believed that without the sacrament of baptism, the natives were as lowly animals and were often treated as such. The power of the Church was absolute and it enforced its dictates with the sword. In New Mexico, this oppression lasted without opposition from the time Coronado led his expedition through the Southwest in 1540 until the Pueblo Revolt in 1680; and then continued after the reconquest. In Florida, the natives fought the Seminole Wars to protest the taking of their lands but in the end they acquiesced or were driven out. The Pueblo Indians succeeded for a short time in taking back New Mexico. This was the only successful revolt in North America by native people. In Florida, the Spaniards had their hands full with the French and especially the British who would use the Creek Indians to drive out the Spaniards. To complicate matters, the Seminole Indians would help the runaway African slaves by hiding them in their villages. The British, not as heavy-handed as the Spaniards, would achieve in trade what the Spaniards wanted to achieve by force – an acceptable relationship with the Indians.

Because of outside influences, Florida developed quickly and was able to exploit its natural resources. New Mexico, at the time it became a territory of the United States, was essentially as it had been in the sixteen hundreds – undeveloped. When Mexico declared its independence from Spain in 1821, both New Mexico and Texas began to test the resolve of their new patrons. The United States Army of the West took New Mexico under the leadership of General Stephen Watts Kearny without firing a shot. Texas proved to be a more difficult acquisition with the Mexican attack on the Alamo and the subsequent battle of San Jacinto.

Many residents in New Mexico still use the Spanish language on a daily basis. The religion is still mainly Catholic. Although Florida has indeed a large Catholic population, the various Protestant denominations make up greater numbers overall. This is due to the heavy immigration from the northern states, which was primarily Protestant. While Florida had no difficulty being admitted as a state to the Union, New Mexico was one of the last territories to be admitted to the Union, despite its many petitions over the years. Even after Florida had seceded from the Union prior to the Civil War, it had comparatively little difficulty returning to the fold. New Mexico, on the other hand, was considered a foreign country and was denied statehood until 1912.

The establishment of the railroads played an enormous role in both New Mexico and Florida as well as in the rest of the nation. With New Mexico, it meant the end of the Santa Fe Trail and its wagon trains over hostile Indian territory. With Florida, it meant the development of the southern part of the peninsula, its land sale booms and population growth.

During the Civil War, both Texas and Florida fought on the side of the Confederacy while New Mexico remained loyal to the Union. On seceding from the Union, Texas tried to fulfill its dream of making the Rio Grande its western boundary by invading New Mexico. Albuquerque and Santa Fe fell quickly but the Battle of Glorieta proved to be fatal for the Texans. Florida, wanting to preserve its status as a slave-owning state fought on the side of the South. Florida served as a supplier of food for the Confederate armies.

Today, despite similar origins, the former Spanish regions are very different. California drew thousands of settlers during the gold rush and kept them there with the bountiful soil, gentle climate and the sea. Texas, with its vast plains, its cattle ranches and oil fields is today a prosperous state. New Mexico remains one of the poorest states in the nation. It has little natural wealth, although gold and silver have been mined there. Because of its arid land, in constant need of rain as it most certainly was during the time of the early Spaniards, the state cannot coax much from the desert soil. Florida, on the other hand, due to its excellent weather (despite the propensity for hurricanes), its magnificent coastline and ample water supply has become an international mecca for tourism. While it may be true that state budgets are always in need of more funds than they possess, Florida has the wherewithal to thrive and continue to draw thousands of visitors each year.

It is important that we continue to ask about our past as well as our future, not only on a state-by-state basis but through a comparative lens which further enriches our understanding of our national heritage.

Printed in the United States
87022LV00005B/305/A

9 780865 344563